Double Vision
My Life in Film

ANDRZEJ WAJDA

Translated by
Rose Medina

faber and faber
LONDON · BOSTON

First published in Great Britain
in 1989 by Faber and Faber Limited
3 Queen Square London WCIN 3AU
This edition published in 1990
First published in the USA in 1989
by Henry Holt and Company, Inc., New York
and simultaneously in Canada
by Fitzhenry & Whiteside Limited, Ontario
Originally published in French
as *Un Cinema Nommé Désir*
by Editions Stock, Paris

Printed in England by Clays Ltd, St Ives plc

Copyright © 1986 by Editions Stock
Translation copyright © Faber and Faber Limited 1989

A CIP record for this book is available
from the British Library

ISBN 0-571-15350-X

To my wife, Krystyna

Contents

1

Who Is This Book For?

As I was writing this book I often asked myself who it was intended for. Partway through I realized that it was intended for me.

I was twenty-four when I interrupted my study of painting at the Academy of Fine Arts in Cracow to take up cinema. Today, after more than thirty years of work, I have decided to tell that incredibly naive young man that I was in 1949 all that I have learned, all that I have come to understand since. That is why I shall refrain from talking about other people's experiences and limit myself to what I have been able to clarify in my own mind in the process of making films, directing plays, and working in television.

My own experience relates first and foremost to what I have accomplished in my own country. I had the great good luck to be present at the beginning of filmmaking in Poland, to help it gain acceptance with the Polish public, and to make Polish films known and appreciated abroad. In 1981, our film industry produced forty films and as many made-for-television movies. When I first started working in film, the total industry produced five to seven pictures per year. Television did not yet exist. In Poland, the movie industry is completely nationalized, from the production on through the distribution. Is there any point, therefore, in reading my book in those parts of the world where filmmaking is completely separate from state control, and subject only to free-market conditions? I think there is. Throughout the world state interference in filmmaking is increasing. In many places the state finances films in whole or in part and never completely disinterestedly.

In the course of these thirty-plus years, the world has changed completely. The constant fear of a global war, which could break out at any time and in any place, has made us much more observant and aware of other people's lives, since our lives may well depend on what they do or don't do. . . .

If you want to know the truth about another country, who is in a better position to tell it than an eyewitness? And we film-makers are especially privileged in being able to offer through our vision and our films the truth of distant countries that too few are familiar with.

Right after World War II, our vision of the outside world was influenced primarily by American films. We learned of England's battle against Hitler through *Mrs. Miniver*, the cruelties of the Japanese from *Bridge on the River Kwai*, and Germany after the defeat from *Trial at Nuremberg*. Not long afterward we began to see the war in a whole other light, through such films as Roberto Rossellini's *Open City* and René Clément's *The Battle of the Rails*. Here it was not Hollywood re-creating reality but aspects of the war filmed right on the scene of the crime.

It is in the context of these last two films that mine appeared: *Kanal* and *Ashes and Diamonds*. Both pictures spoke for a country that was just beginning to exist on the map of the film world. Our pictures could not compare to French or Italian films of the same period: they were made with modest means, and our actors were unknown. And yet with all their imperfections they did offer the truth of an eyewitness account.

I sense that today in a number of countries there is a desire for an indigenous cinema that would depict and accurately portray the life-style of that country, with all its joys, conflicts, and concerns. This book is above all addressed to the young people of those countries. And what about the others? My hope is that other readers will nonetheless find in these pages some basic truths about the art of filmmaking, independent of geography and politics. For in my experience, there are certain rules and restrictions that are universally applicable.

In writing this book I have tried to follow the basic stages one goes through in the process of making a film, from the birth of the idea in the director's head through the written scenario, the shooting, the editing, on up to the premiere.

For better or worse, I have decided not to eliminate any of the mundane details of these various steps, all those "obvious" elements that every filmmaker knows automatically. The fact is, those so-called obvious aspects of filmmaking were what gave me the most trouble when I first started out.

2

The Hardest
Part Is the Idea Itself

How can one define the "idea for a film"? Nothing is more difficult. We say: "I have an idea!" Or: "My idea is . . ." Or: "The way I see it is . . ." If you choose as your subject a novel everybody knows, is that the same as an idea for a film?

No, making up one's mind to turn *War and Peace* into a film is not the same thing as having an idea. And yet my reasons for wanting to adapt Tolstoy's novel to the screen, and the way I want to do it, might well constitute a valid film "idea." The infinite richness of the novel lends itself to any number of interpretations. All great works of literature have long lives because each new generation, each new period, finds something new and different in them. Thus our job with such works is to discover what it is about them that will truly interest people today when the film comes out.

What is the immortal idea of *Antigone*? It is she, Antigone, a weak-natured woman who nonetheless is incredibly strong because of her innate character. Antigone incarnates and defends the eternal laws of nature against the encroachment of temporal laws imposed by those in power. Our job is to find the thread that will explain and express that idea as beautifully as possible.

Hard by the city walls, two brothers in opposite camps meet in battle. Both are killed, but whereas one is given a hero's funeral, the other is denied burial rites. Although Creon, the king of the city, has forbidden it, Antigone decides to defy the king's prohibition and bury her brother herself. That drama, that defiance, does indeed bring out the character of Antigone.

In his version of the story, Sophocles joins heaven and earth, gods and men. Anyone who remakes or adapts *Antigone* today has to take that situation into account. He or she has to believe that above this earth are gods whose laws determine the lives of the people below.

All I mean by that is that any anecdote, any story told around a table, any news item read in the paper or heard on the street, may well contain the elements of tragedy worthy of Sophocles. But one has to take that snippet and ferret out its deeper meaning, figure out who the real hero is, and in so doing determine the narrator's viewpoint. It is true that the king Creon is as tragic a figure as Antigone: his wife turns away from him, he loses his son, the city condemns him. But that is not the subject of *Antigone*. By the same token, the hero of *Ashes and Diamonds* is not the Party Secretary Szczuka—who was indeed the hero of the novel from which the film was taken—but his assassin, Maciek Chelmicki. Why? Because Creon's reasons are only revealed through Antigone, Szczuka's through Maciek Chelmicki. The choice of Maciek Chelmicki as the hero of the film *Ashes and Diamonds* was the first element of my "idea."

The action of Jerzy Andrzejewski's novel, *Ashes and Diamonds*, took place over roughly a two-week period in May 1945, at the end of the war. The film, on the other hand, takes place in a little over twenty-four hours: one day and night, and into dawn of the following day. I sensed that the situating of the action during this final night of the war and the dawn of the first day of peace, with all the hopes engendered by that situation, coupled with everything that would go toward destroying those hopes, would have an unexpected shock effect on the viewer. My "idea" of the film, therefore, stems from only these two decisions, made before the script was written.

Let's take another example, that of an original idea conceived especially for the cinema. What must it contain? What is needed to create the dynamic tension? To my mind, it is a conflict specifically created among the various characters. I've always thought that this conflict is all the more violent if it occurs within a family and not among strangers. Ties of blood are the strongest, and not only in primitive societies. The viewers will understand the duties of a son to his father, the feelings of a mother for her children, and all the conflicts that those sentiments can create. In fact, because the viewers can understand and relate so intimately to such situations, their participation in the film will be all the more personal.

3

Life Is Rich in Ideas

Several years ago I visited a housing development that was under construction. I found its uniformity depressing. Later on, I saw a number of similar developments and I was always struck by the notion that such a site could be not only a background for a film, but also a place rich in unique human dramas. Unfortunately, though, I was never able to find a plot that would have conveyed that action to the screen.

Several years passed, until one day in Moscow I saw a housing development not unlike the ones I had seen in Poland. I was told the following story about it. A young actor was shooting a film on a Moscow street when a young woman passed by. They struck up a conversation, liked each other, and a few days later he escorted her home. They spent the night together—a very exciting, wonderful night, according to the person telling the story—and in the morning the young actor got up and went out to buy some things for breakfast while the woman was still asleep. But as he happily started back to the apartment, he got lost in the maze of the identical buildings, and however hard he tried to retrace his steps he could never find the door that opened to what he thought of as his new life.

Ever since I heard that story I looked upon these ghostly conglomerations of buildings as more than a mere backdrop for a possible film. They became a film in themselves. What is a succession of identical houses, hallways, doors, and windows? Nothing more than the proof that such uniformity exists and creates fear. Not the architecture itself, but the drama of a man who is the victim of this architecture can affect and move the spectator.

Another example. In every country of the world, the powers that be have various means of ascertaining what people are thinking. But in our system in Poland none of these sources is reliable. No one in his right mind would report to the authorities things they wouldn't want to hear. That is why the first news concerning the general strike that paralyzed the country in 1980 came not from the press but from the electrical generators that supplied the country: from hour to hour there was a steady decrease in electricity consumed, from which we deduced that the factories had ceased to operate and that we had better be ready for anything.

Think of all the dialogues, all the shots a director would have needed to make the audience understand that a general strike was imminent—whereas the scene of revealing it via the surprise of an immediate decrease in electricity generated gets the message across immediately and dramatically, with all the sociological factors implicit in that situation.

Unfortunately, I didn't know this when I made *Man of Iron*, and consequently that film has an overlong introduction with many, many scenes instead of one single scene showing how a journalist doing an article on the electricity supply becomes an eyewitness to the unexpected drop in power. He is the one (and the audience along with him) who learns what is going on in the country, the events that will be the film's point of departure. But I missed out on this opportunity for a short, beautiful, and forceful introduction.

Seizing and recording anecdotes of this kind are an essential part of any director's work. It is through such anecdotes that the general becomes specific, the abstract concrete, and the idea incarnate as a human drama.

Another example: the French Revolution at the end of the Reign of Terror. The streets are alive with people. On the balconies above, the women watch as the cart bearing the grim Robespierre to his death passes beneath them. Suddenly, as if one, the women all tear open their corsets and reveal their breasts. Through this presumably spontaneous gesture of protest, these women also unknowingly created a new mood, announcing the advent of an era of liberated morals.

If you know scenes like these and if you succeed in incorporating them in your script, they will tell the viewer more than the most convincing dialogues a scriptwriter can ever dream up. Major social tensions often unfold by gestures or movements that the scriptwriter would be hard-pressed to invent.

My 1957 film *Kanal* is the true story of someone who took part in the 1944 Warsaw uprising. Yet during the Cannes Film Festival, a Hollywood scriptwriter congratulated our scriptwriter, Jerzy Stawinski, on the unusual power of his imagination. For him it was unthinkable that the canals were the only means of communication since the streets were the scene of constant gunfire.

Let's consider this from a slightly different point of view. I have a dog. Several years ago I was going through a very hard time professionally. The minister of cinematography had decided to do me in, having made up his mind that I was the main obstacle standing in the way of his realizing certain film projects. (He was not far wrong.) It was at this time that my dog fell seriously ill. I called the veterinarian and asked him to come over right away. He examined my poor dog carefully, looked at me, and said, "If you don't manage to calm down and get control of yourself, it will be the end of your dog." I was overwhelmed with a double fear: for my dog and myself. Till then I had been quite convinced that the minister in question was losing his mind because of my stubbornness, whereas I, of course, was in perfect control of myself.

Picture the scene: the actor looks at his dog who has figured out his secret. Little by little he becomes aware of his own malaise: his hands shake, his stomach is all knotted up, he begins to suffer from dizzy spells. The conversation between man and dog can be turned into a brilliant piece of bravura by the scriptwriter, and lo and behold the dog becomes part of cinematic history.

A well-placed anecdote, neatly situated where the film demands it, can sum up in a moment what we might otherwise have to construct out of any number of tedious descriptive scenes.

This kind of reflection on a script will enable you to determine from a completed film how much credit should go to the script and how much to the actors' interpretation. This gives rise to all sorts of misunderstandings: the audience is moved by the actors' performance but what really affects them deeply is the story of Antigone's fate, as told by Sophocles.

4

Where's the Subject?

The long months spent working out the details of the script obscure the true contours of the conflict one wants to express on the screen via the characters. How can one preserve a constant freshness while working on an anecdote one knows by heart? There is only one way to do it: forget the anecdote!

When I was working on *Hamlet* for the theater, I realized that the hardest thing was to relate onstage the sequence of events in proper order, from Hamlet's first meeting with his mother and the king to Fortinbras' victorious entrance in the final scene. That sequence of events could have been different if:

1. Hamlet had come to terms with his uncle the king.
2. He had refused to believe in his father's ghost.
3. He had not succumbed to Ophelia's charms.
4. He had succeeded in killing the king while he was at prayer.
5. He had not killed Polonius by mistake, thinking he was the king.

Plus a whole host of other "ifs.". . .

And yet despite that seemingly whimsical, arbitrary quality (or perhaps because of it), we have to admit that *Hamlet* has a steel-like logic to its construction that leads the Danish prince inexorably to his death.

What would our own lives be worth if we knew the details of our final moment? If that were the case, we would have to make every action and every word concur with our death. It would be unbearable. The same is true for Hamlet. What does it matter that everyone in the audience knows Hamlet's destiny? What really interests them onstage is what this "poor boy" will do to save his life, to triumph in the end.

The best method of construction I've come up with is to go over a scene in my mind constantly, telling myself what I am doing as I direct. The very process of telling myself the story over and over forces me to eliminate unnecessary details. I emphasize what seems to me essential. To keep the audience on its toes I heighten the effect, multiply the abrupt changes and the surprises, and discover in each scene its main theme and its meaning. The same kind of exercise needs to be done with one's own memory. Whatever the memory fails to retain is secondary. You can eliminate it from the script. The scriptwriter has to tell his story in a few sentences. Listen to Aristotle's summary, in the *Poetics*, of Homer's *Odyssey*, a long, fourteen-part poem:

> For many years a man wanders across the face of the earth, far from his native land, completely alone though watched over by the god Poseidon. Back home his fortune is being squandered by various interlopers and his son has become the victim of their plots. Battered by storms, he finally arrives home, reveals his identity to some close friends, then launches an attack against his enemies, finally crushing them and winning the day.

Doesn't this "treatment" capture the story's essentials?

Any subject can be approached from a variety of different

12

viewpoints which cast a new light on it. But let us come back to *Hamlet*. The basic Hamlet story—its characters and plot—were well known long before Shakespeare's time. *Hamlet*'s originality does not lie, therefore, in the bare bones of the story itself. Hamlet needed a motive, an "ideology." It's easy to say: "I'm going to kill!" But bringing oneself to do it is another matter: what an effort it is to convince oneself that it is unavoidable. No such inexorable quality existed in the earlier versions of *Hamlet*, and what is more, the story itself did not require it.

Another example. If I am relating the story of two lovers and in the opening scene show them in bed together, the audience knows that they will stay with the couple until the end of the film, unless something serious intervenes to separate them. But in that case, this "something" will be the subject of the film.

How stunned everyone was at the Cannes Film Festival when we watched Michelangelo Antonioni's film *L'Avventura* and realized that Marcello Mastroianni had "lost" his partner and had simply ceased to be interested in her. She didn't reappear until the very end of the film. The effect was both shocking and magnificent. That day the world of film was freed of one more of its preconceived notions. And yet the rest of *L'Avventura* derives from what I might term ordinary fiction; it is not really different from other films of the same kind. Only a viewpoint taken to its ultimate conclusion can lead to a true innovation.

Where is the subject of a film situated? To find out you must read the script closely and carefully, from every angle, first of all adopting the viewpoint of each of the major characters.

A fresh look at the location where the action of a film takes place can also be considered an innovation. I was delighted and intrigued by that street scene in *The French Connection* with automobiles rushing by, their multicolored bodies glistening, reflections in store windows, red lights changing on the street corners, flashes of neon going on and off. It was hard to make out anything distinctly in that confusion. What is the subject of the film? Investigation, inquiry. This opening image of the city transcends the interest it may have provoked in the mind of the viewer: rather, it expresses the essence of the film itself.

Another example of what I might call this search for the subject within the given elements of the drama or story: Jerzy Stawinski, the author of *Kanal*, wrote another screenplay hard on the heels of the success of that earlier film. The new script was entitled *The Assassination Attempt*, and was based on the true story of an assassination attempt on Reinhard Heydrich, the head of the SS and the German police in Warsaw. The director, Andrzej Munk, liked the script and wanted to make the film, but didn't do it in the end. Eventually it was made by Passendorfer, another director. After opening night, Munk gave me his version of *The Assassination Attempt*. On the surface, the story he told was the same as the movie we had just seen. It is dawn. The members of the Resistance movement are saying good-bye to their families and loved ones. They take up their posts along the route where Heydrich's motorcade is supposed to pass. Time drags on; the motorcade has been delayed. Finally, the leader of the Resistance group gives the signal: he doffs his hat. Up to this point, everything is following Stawinski's semidocumentary script. But here Munk's version differs: after the signal is given, nobody shoots. The car passes beneath the eyes of the would-be assassins. The tension becomes unbearable. The car moves away, farther and farther. . . . Now the Resistance chief calls his men together and says: "All right, tomorrow, same time, same spot." We realize that we have just witnessed not the attempt itself but the dress rehearsal.

Let's take a look at the two versions. Munk is not telling the story of the attempted assassination itself, so carefully reconstructed by Stawinski. He is taking things further and opting for a whole other subject: the film as he saw it was not about the attempted assassination but about the psychological processes people have to go through to overcome their fear. If the dress rehearsal was so stressful and demanding, what about the event itself? The subject is no longer: "Who will kill whom?" but "How will it get done?"

In my early days as a filmmaker, I made a documentary about the excellent Polish sculptor Xawery Dunikowski. In those days we had a fairly clear, precise idea about how such a film should be made. I focused my attention on the sculptures themselves, shooting them from various angles to show them to best effect, being as "original" as I knew how. In my mind, the background played an important role in the process. Thus I placed a group of sculptures representing "pregnant women" on the beach. The sea lapped at their feet; nearby a naked child played with the seashells in the sand. These "artistic" images were accompanied by background music and a poetic commentary recited voice-over by an actor who was barely restraining his emotion. In other words, it was a typical film about art, as we conceived the genre in those days.

Dunikowski himself was a fascinating man: something of an adventurer, he had traveled widely. He had also spent four years in Auschwitz, and in fact had been one of its original inmates. As the days rolled by and Dunikowski watched our laborious efforts to portray his work to good advantage, he was clearly bored with the whole proceeding, and started talking nonstop about himself. His stories, as well as the way he told them, were utterly fascinating to me. But I was so wrapped up in what I was doing that I didn't have time to realize the opportunity being offered to me. I was one step away from making a key discovery! But it's very difficult to maintain a freshness of vision, so that you really see the possibilities in what is around you, all the while concentrating on the shooting. If I had taken the opportunity then to film Dunikowski, I would have been ahead of my time in making *cinéma vérité,* for which we had to wait another several years.

One of the greatest obstacles to filmmaking is making sure, in the preparation as well as in the shooting and editing, that you don't get bogged down, spending too much time on useless scenes, superfluous dialogues, or pointless episodes. By that I don't mean that a cleverly constructed play or highly crafted script is the ideal. Not at all. Any work of art has to contain a certain margin of the gratuitous: the artist must always have the possibility to express himself freely vis-à-vis his subject. Here I am looking for an answer to the question of just what, during the shooting of a film, should (or could) be developed or extended, as well as what should (or could) be compressed or perhaps eliminated altogether in the editing room.

When Antigone is sentenced to death by Creon, and her fate is sealed, Sophocles brings her back onstage to bid farewell to life, which in relation to the action of the play is a speech that could well be judged both overly long and even superfluous. And yet the audience listens to her with rapt attention, because:

1. They feel a profound compassion for Antigone, whose reasons and motives for doing what she has done they fully understand.
2. They hope that something unforeseen will occur that will save her at the last moment.

I think that example is worth thinking about. Every director who is in the middle of shooting a film is full of ideas that he would dearly love to see on-screen. That's what gives a film the stamp of individuality. The only problem is, all too often these ideas are either in conflict with the thrust or action of the film itself, or are purely decorative. Many directors, especially in the early stages of their careers, are blinded by the love they feel for these ideas that are too good to pass up and devote too much

16

time and energy to making sure they find their place in the film. They then find themselves with not enough time for what is really indispensable. Yet these ideas can be turned to good advantage if they are integrated into the action of the film in a meaningful way and placed so that rather than becoming an obstacle, they support the essential message you want to express.

5

The Traps of a Script

There is nothing more dangerous than what I call an "impressionistic script," describing a film that the scriptwriter already "sees" in his mind. More often than not, such a script is closed, ready-made. In all probability the only person who could make such a film is the scriptwriter himself, for it is woven with the threads of his own sensibility. As a director, I have a feeling when presented with such a situation, that the author is asking the impossible from me. That film, which I have not yet seen in my mind's eye, cannot be a point of departure for me. Unfortunately, most film scripts written by amateurs fall into this category.

Please don't misunderstand. I am not advising directors to reject scripts that are difficult or even seemingly impenetrable. But I do distrust hermetic projects, based on sensations rather than human characters and action that develops the characters and makes them believable.

You could make a film from the newspaper, from a simple news item. Someone committed suicide. Why? The answer could well be fascinating. The very question implies an action, a film. Yes, but . . .

One must be very careful with inspiration of this kind. The

action may be implicit in the news item, but the director's task is to ferret out what that news item means; in other words, to find the subject of his film, just as, for *Madame Bovary*, Flaubert was able to discern the theme of women's liberation in a news item.

Many fledgling scriptwriters think that a precise and detailed description of what the actors should do from scene to scene protects the author from the whims and arbitrary decisions of a director. Nothing could be more wrong. Just think of *Antigone*! Sophocles did nothing more than give a few parenthetical instructions, because Antigone's character is so perfectly expressed in the dialogue, and in the action itself. That is why no director on earth, young or old, stupid or brilliant, can ever ruin *Antigone*. Nor can any actress, bad or good, completely betray the basic sense of the character she is portraying.

Any description of how the actors should perform is inevitably based on actors the scriptwriter has already seen. The problem is, nothing is more tenuous or transitory than styles of acting. Just look at descriptions of Eleonora Duse or Sarah Bernhardt, or the Russian actors and actresses of Stanislavsky. The methods of another period are no longer convincing in our own time. Shakespeare gave us no directions about how his characters should be played, but an actor who manages to seize the essence of Macbeth will never confuse his character with that of Henry IV or Othello.

I have always known, whenever I looked at reproductions of Da Vinci's *Last Supper*, that he had put into that painting a mysterious hand armed with a knife, a hand that belonged to none of the characters seated behind the table. Not long ago I studied the passage in the Gospels that refers to that mysterious hand (Luke 22: 21–23): "But, Behold, the hand of him that betrayeth me is with me on the table." Is there any way of expressing that thought more forcefully, more truthfully? Jesus

19

does not yet tell us to whom that hand belongs. It is "with me on the table." How clear and how obvious! I think that directors who are adapting classical works to the screen should take a lesson from that example, and read their authors as closely as Leonardo read the Gospels. In so doing they will have quenched their thirst from the same source.

6

The Art of Dialogue

When I was a young man dialogue in film was considered a necessary evil. Whenever you found yourself incapable of expressing yourself visually you inserted a verbal exchange. For years people kept telling us how terrible the dialogue was in Polish films—and they were right. And how poorly Polish actors spoke on-screen—and there again they were right. Today all that has changed: Polish films are as eloquent as any in the world. The directors Bajon, Holland, Kieslowski, Zanussi, Marczewski write their own film dialogues, bearing in mind the action of the film, its characters, and the actors who speak the lines.

Thanks to their efforts Polish filmgoers are no longer resistant to the idea of hearing Polish on-screen. Their earlier resistance was because they rarely heard Polish spoken in movies. The cinema of our youth spoke American, French, or Italian. What a shock and surprise it was to us when Ingmar Bergman appeared and introduced to us a tongue nobody knew. Three, then five or six or seven films per year were not enough to convince the Polish public that their language was suited to the screen. I believe that the introduction of the Polish language to the cinema around the world is, from our point of view, one of the most important cultural elements of the postwar era.

The dialogue of any film requires a writer. A film writer whose job is to write dialogue, or polish someone else's, is no solution. The fact is, real film writers are a rarity—which explains why film directors resort to all kinds of subterfuge in their efforts to circumvent the problem. If the film is an adaptation from a literary work, the script most often simply picks up dialogues from the book. The problem is, those dialogues were written to be read, and very often don't ring true on-screen. Film directors often grind the originals to dust or rewrite them with the actors, in a sense, trying them on for size depending on their various talents. Others do their best to improvise dialogue right on the set, simply providing the actors with a few rather general ideas. The problem with this is, instead of natural conversation that moves the action forward or at the very least fits in with the thrust and movement of the film, improvised dialogues often degenerate into repetition and nonsensical exchanges, not all that different from the inanities of a couple of drunks. Few and far between are those actors who know how to improvise monologues or exchanges where the director's will, the actors' own personalities, and those of the characters they are portraying meld into a meaningful whole. One successful example of that method working beautifully occurred in my film Birchwood, where Daniel Olbrychski is talking with his daughter. Halfway through the film Olbrychski understood clearly who he was and what his character wanted, and this enabled him to improvise brilliantly, aided by the fact that his daughter was totally ignorant of what he was talking about and therefore could not respond to any of his questions.

Yet there are certain exchanges that no actor, assistant director, or director can improvise. I think for example of the following exchange:

POLICEMAN: How old are you?
BOY: A hundred years old.
POLICEMAN (*slapping him*): How old are you?
BOY: A hundred and one.

No actor could have come up with that on the spur of the moment. It takes a real writer—in this instance Jerzy Andrzejewski, the author of *Ashes and Diamonds*.

In their search for naturalness, film writers too often have reduced dialogue to noise, to one more part of the sound track. They do their best to convince us directors that any other form of dialogue is outmoded. The only problem is, that lack of differentiation in most film dialogues stems from the *quality*—or lack of quality—of what their authors have to say: directors, deprived of dialogues that would move the action forward, are in turn reduced to juggling with *conversations* that at most suggest the atmosphere of the film. In a good script, all you really need to do is read the dialogues themselves, skipping the rest of the text (I advise anyone interested in making a film to try that experiment before committing himself): the dialogues in and of themselves will, in a good script, suffice to give you a good idea of the film's subject and action.

In my experience the best dialogues are written by dramatists. And yet they often don't work as well in films as the dialogues taken from novels. The reason, I believe, is that a work written for the stage has to conform to certain theatrical conventions. Even the dramatists who are considered "naturalists" are subject to this problem. Stage conventions demand a strict interdependence between what is said and the action of the play, which allows the author to situate the work in a couple of sets. Given

23

this, it is superfluous to "show" what is going on offstage. In the final scene of Chekhov's *The Three Sisters* would the sight of an infantry regiment crossing the stage add to or intensify the sisters' longing for another life? A "vignette" such as that might well be lovely, but it would also be useless. Plays do not need the air and space that films do by definition, for their dialogues evoke the image of the world that films have to depict on the screen.

7

The
Shooting Script,
Yesterday and Today

I think a history of the cinema could be written by following the
evolution of how films were shot, and more specifically, by following the technical improvements in the sensitivity of film itself.
That evolution had a far greater impact on filmmaking than one
might believe.

When I started making films some thirty years ago, there was
a very simple equation: interior scenes had to be shot in a studio
and exterior shots had to have sunlight. Over the past several
years I've only done trial shots in studios. Nowadays films can
be shot virtually anywhere the action calls for: in apartments, in
factories, newspaper offices, you name it. This new freedom stems
directly from the improved sensitivity of the film itself from one
year to the next.

When I was making *Kanal* in 1957, I had to build an immense
jumble of streets and doorways, of canals of varying dimensions.
I had to figure out my camera angles and distances for each setup
far in advance and keep my production designer constantly in-
formed as the action progressed from scene to scene, since he
had to plan ahead for the placement of the lighting equipment
concealed in the walls of the set. I spent endless hours preparing

the shooting script, down to the tiniest details, knowing that there was no room for the unforeseen to creep in and translate itself to the screen. I sketched the working drawings and the set designs myself, with a corresponding camera angle for each, and then oversaw the construction in collaboration with the chief cameraman Jerzy Lipman, verifying that all was exactly as called for by checking everything through the viewfinder of the camera.

Slightly more than fifteen years later, in 1973, we made *Promised Lands*. The film took place both in sumptuous private homes and in dingy factories, both of which still exist in Lodz. We placed strong lights above the looms of the textile factories, lighting the enormous mill, which employed over a thousand workers on a shift. No longer did we need the minutely detailed shooting script that I had put together for *Kanal*. Our script moved from scene to scene, according to the location we had chosen, and that was enough. Thus, for me, there was a complete evolution in the art of writing a shooting script between *Kanal* and *Promised Lands*.

That evolution is more generally linked to changes in ways of direction that evolved through the decades. In the early days of film, before the "talkies," there was what I would call "dynamic editing," that is, short takes where the missing sound had to be made up for by the action itself. Then, in the early days of sound movies, we had all those static shots, usually long or very long shots that went on forever and were forever boring. Directors in those days had to make up ridiculous situations so that the scene could be shot from one end to the other without moving the camera.

In the 1950s, when I first started making films, we used to celebrate the hundredth take. Today nobody is even aware when you reach the five-hundredth take. The number of takes per film has grown enormously. A full-length feature, which used to consist of perhaps two to three hundred takes, today has from seven hundred to a thousand on the average.

In the not-too-distant past the shooting script was more or less cast in stone. It took into account every last detail of what you might need during the shooting of the film. Everything, from the length of each shot to the exact placement of the music.

All that is a thing of the past. Today the scriptwriter tries to include everything required right in the text, rather than having all sorts of technical marginalia outside the script proper, so that the action flows along consistently with the meaning and rhythm of his story. Scenes are no longer divided into predetermined shots arranged sequentially; the director and chief cameraman can pick and choose the sequence they prefer in the course of shooting. No longer do we worry about how long each shot is; what matters is the length of the scene itself, and in due course we pass on any supplementary indications to the assistant directors to act upon.

The text of a script or shooting script is clear. It allows you to follow both story line and the course of the action. It does not preempt or prejudge the direction, which can be shifted as necessary to suit the location, the unpredictable shifts in weather, the frame of mind of the actors that day, and a whole host of other elusive elements that on-screen will give the audience the sense that you have captured life in all its uncertain and unpredictable truth. It is not all that difficult to describe the film *Alexander Nevsky*, with its static frames, as almost photographically perfect. But try to do the same thing with almost any contemporary film, a collage of hundreds of barely discernible shots, such as *The French Connection*! Here the director is no longer dealing with framing but with sharp, rapid, virtually elusive "glances" that the audience may miss if they're not on their toes. And yet, still today when I'm thinking about or planning a given scene, which I see clearly in my own mind, I try to work out the various shots in sequence and draw up a blueprint of the whole scene before shooting commences. I give all these sheets of paper as well as all my other notes to the assistant directors, because at the time of shooting I want to approach that same scene with a free hand and my mind completely open to anything that might strike me on the set.

Some directors learn their shooting scripts by heart. They are wrong. The shooting script is useful in indicating the general direction a film will take, but it should not be thought of as a four-lane highway. Otherwise you're leaving yourself no margin for the unexpected: those sudden possibilities that occur because of the actors themselves, the weather, or any number of other obstacles that arise on the spot that have to be dealt with. The road followed by the film may turn into a winding path or disappear into the woods. There is no longer any map. In order not to lose his way, the director has to rely on the compass that consists of the basic plot and premise of the film, the story and anecdotal material that move that plot along: who is doing what, in relation to whom, and to what purpose? All throughout the shooting I keep asking the crew: what happens next? Remind me how it all turns out. That's how I keep myself on track.

8

The Most Original Spectacle

For the most part television is merely the medium that transmits other genres—plays, films—through a new technology. And yet it is also the originator of a new dramatic spectacle accessible to millions around the world: major sports such as football, tennis, sumo wrestling in Japan. Everyone knows the rules; each spectator can check the decision of the officials. And above all, the committed spectator can become an ardent fan of one of the teams. In fact if you don't, you may as well turn off the set before you die of boredom. What's playing on the set before our very eyes is real life, because we don't know the final outcome. But aside from sports, is there any possibility that this new genre, television, might blossom in the same way in other areas? Could there ever be a television equivalent of *Antigone*?

Some years back I was in Algiers. One of the local filmmakers told me the following true story, which to my mind represents that unattainable ideal of an authentic television drama.

It took place the day the French officially left Algiers, abandoning the city to its fate. The entire population took to the streets and, in the course of events, still in a state of euphoria, arrived at the television studios. The gaping, empty studios, the

29

television cameras and equipment scattered here and there, did not in the minds of the surging crowd seem to have any connection with what they conceived as television—that is, at least until the moment when someone in the know plugged in the cameras. Suddenly the blank screens of the monitors lit up, and the demonstrators saw their own bodies and faces on-screen. At first they were amused. Then they were emboldened. Hey, we're on TV! They realized if they could see themselves on the monitors, the rest of the population could also see them on sets throughout the city. Maybe even farther. If that's true, they thought, then we should make good use of the opportunity: so they began to sing, dance, recite. The result was a long, uninterrupted television show that for once was completely authentic. It finally ended, as do all such spontaneous demonstrations, with the arrival of the police and armed forces. They unplugged the cameras, dispersed the "performers," and to make sure everyone understood that the state had things under control, they officially sealed off the studios.

If only television had existed at the time of the French Revolution—audiences in 1789 might have been able to see on-screen the storming of the Bastille—not to mention a few other key dates of recorded history! But as the captions of so many engravings from the nineteenth century noted: "There was no photographer present." Even today, there are too many occasions when "no television cameras were there" because the authorities clamped down in time.

I think of the possibilities of such a program when I watch those futuristic films in which man is the prey, pursued by hunters armed with cameras. What a dismal thought! That is the antithesis of the spontaneous demonstrations put on by the Algerian people the day of their liberation.

9

Casting Comes from Inspiration

A theater lover once said to me: "Anyone who works with untalented actors is committing a double error. First, you are wasting your time. Second, you're depriving the talented actors you're not working with."

There are only two moments when inspiration (a sudden illumination or insight) is indispensable to a director. One is the moment when you first see clearly the "idea" or premise of the picture. The other is when you choose your actors. Obviously, that inspiration is circumscribed by the availability of actors you're considering. To do your job right in casting a film, you really have to do your homework well in advance: see lots of films, go to the theater as often as you can, haunt acting studios, keep in touch with what amateur acting groups are doing. Your range has to include the most lavish productions and the most modest provincial offerings. No film or talent agency can ever do the job for you. In fact, it takes years for a director to amass in his or her mind the file of possibilities. I cannot stress the importance of this aspect of filmmaking: you really have to see everything. But you must also be careful not to look so far afield that you pass up some possibility right in your own backyard. In *Ashes*

31

and Diamonds I found the right foil for the sometimes exaggerated mobility and spontaneity of Cybulski in the person of Adam Pawlikowski, a man of untold talents, a musician, writer, and critic—in other words, the eternal Renaissance man. In my first film, *Generation*, he played the ocarina. In *Kanal* he had a minor role as an SS soldier. But in *Ashes and Diamonds* he had a major role, which launched his career. I found Jerzy Radziwillowicz (*Man of Marble*) in a play being performed by the Warsaw Drama School as part of its graduation program. I discovered the actor who played in a particularly affecting episode of the stage version of *Promised Lands* when he was a member of an amateur acting company in Cracow: this was Ryszard Bromowicz, who had been a member of the troupe for years.

For years after I had directed a stage production of *Danton* I had dreamed of turning it into a film. But it was not until I had seen the French actor Gerard Depardieu play Danton onstage that I knew I had to do it, for I realized that I had just seen Danton in the flesh.

The moment a director has a clear idea of what his film is or will be, and certainly by the time he has begun to write the script, he should begin to think about the casting.

I am convinced that casting is a creative act. The director is working with a variable, versatile, capricious, human material, namely actors. If one of them has performed brilliantly in a picture that has just been released, that is no guarantee that he'll still be good tomorrow. His great performance may simply be a stroke of luck, a coincidence that may never happen again. And the reverse is also true. What brilliant cinematic debuts were those of James Dean, of Jean-Pierre Belmondo in *Breathless*, of Giulietta Masina in *La Strada*. But then you have to ask yourself the question: where did these actors come from? Who found them? It had to be the directors who had the insight and intuition to sense the possibilities of these unknowns. I'm sure that the directors' advisors and assistants were betting on actors who were already well known.

Directors rarely appear on-screen themselves. If a director has a close affinity with some particular character in a film, he should look for an actor who is close to him in character, temperament, and physical appearance. This explains why some directors work time and again with certain actors. They grow old together, go through the same stages of life together, and leave the scene as one when their careers are over. I sometimes think of an actor who waits for *his* director to surface, for that moment when the director will see him and say, "That's it! He's the one!" And it fills me with sadness to know that more often than not no such moment will come, no such director ever appear.

In addition to the two or three starring roles in every film, there are a number of character parts or secondary roles. I am convinced that such parts should wherever possible be played by actors with strong personalities, if the parts are to remain etched in the minds of the audience. Thus a part that is barely fleshed out in the script itself can, with the help of a good, creative actor, be made memorable. How many times have I seen on-screen real people who are alive and vital, characters I can still remember and who far outshine the few lines devoted to their part in the script. Such roles are never insignificant. If they turn out that way on-screen, it is because an insensitive director couldn't see their potential. Even if an actor is only on-screen for a few brief moments, the part should be played by an actor whose very presence and personality will make an impact on the audience.

10

You Have to
Believe in Your Actors

No matter which actors the director picks for his film, he must start by believing in them completely. He is the mediator between them and success or failure. A stage actor has the audience to relate and react to. Each night, in collaboration with that audience, he works on and perfects his role. In making a film all he has to react to is that naked eye, the camera, that pile of glass and steel from which he will derive no comfort or joy. This only leaves him the director, to whom he can and must reveal the most secret nooks and crannies of his soul, the deepest recesses of his heart.

Picture a man who leads another man to an open window, gently coaxing him to step up over the window frame and jump from the tenth floor: you can't imagine how wonderful it is to fly through the air! That first man is the good director. He inspires confidence and conviction. When an actor has the good fortune to work with such a director you can be sure his performance will be more than routine. A director who doesn't love actors, who doesn't understand how hard their job is, should choose another profession.

There is a major difference between looking and seeing. The

actor must feel that the director is seeing everything he does, be it in rehearsal or during the shooting. He must know that the director is watching him even when he's telling a joke to the crew in the studio cafeteria.

In the early stages of shooting *Ashes and Diamonds*, Zbyszek Cybulski appeared in a doorway, and he stood there shifting his weight back and forth from one leg to the other, perfectly at ease and completely unaware of what he was doing. "You know," he said, after a long pause, "I feel great today."

I took note of that unconscious good humor, also noting that the way he was shifting his weight, the way he was carrying himself, incarnated to a tee the character he was portraying. I was delighted with him at that moment, and I vaguely understood what message he was trying to convey to me. What would have happened if I had wanted to "direct" him my way, without taking into account his silent message? He would have withdrawn into his shell, leaving me alone right up to the end of the film with my image of Maciek Chelmicki on my hands, unfulfilled.

Chinese merchants, it is said, know that when people speak with a lying tongue their hands speak the truth, because truth is in search of an outlet. This explains why the Chinese use the abacus, why they have all those ivory puzzles: to keep the revealing hands under control.

What a lesson for a director! Nothing is more fascinating than watching a man who allows his emotions to get out of control— and seeing them surface little by little, however hard he tries not to show them. Contrary to words, gestures are always revealing.

In the early part of 1982, after a state of emergency had been declared again, Krystyna Janda had just finished shooting a picture she was making in Paris and had to make up her mind whether she would stay in France or come back to Poland. It was obviously an agonizing choice. She went to a friend we both know, who told me the following story:

Janda had just come into the kitchen. I was baking a cake. She took the bowl from my hands and began to tell me a story, beating the eggs as she talked. She was beating them with such intensity and speed that the children came up to me and whispered in my ear: "What's the matter with Aunt Krystyna?" They had understood that something was bothering her. And they had understood it not from her words, since she in fact had been telling a funny story, but solely from her gestures.

That disagreement between words and gestures is the best way to express a psychological truth. The actor is thus freed from "explaining" anything at all; his behavior is plausible and corresponds to the way we all conceal our inner discords and mask our deepest feelings. Thus these discords and feelings will appear as though "despite himself," which is what gives the perfect illusion of truth on screen.

11

Actions Speak Louder than Words
About the Truth of Actors' Performances

To perform in front of the camera is to act.

Here's what I always say to actors:

Don't talk: act!
Don't rehash the same old things over and over again: attack!
Move from the word to the action.
It's a battle: strike, parry, defend, attack.
Who are your allies?
Who are your opponents?
Never forget that comedy takes place in the present—it's not what's done and gone that matters, it is what is yet to be!

Hamlet's monologues are nothing more than a desperate effort to act, even before the action commences. Playing Hamlet in this way allows the actor to breathe new life into the classic role. It is said: paint from life. In 1863 Edouard Manet showed his *Olympia* to the Parisian public, who reacted with shock and indignation. Why? Because instead of painting "femininity," he had dared to paint a woman. The notion of nudity was accepted in those days, but the public could not accept the concrete por-

37

trayal of a *living* naked woman. In working on a role, both actor and director have to think of that analogy, and do their best to emulate it, so that the character is in the same sense concrete.

An actor will play true if he finds himself in a true situation. It is easy to arrive at the truth where the action is violent.

The same cannot be said for psychological truth: it's up to the director to reveal that to the actors. No overrefined speeches, please. The eloquent director loves to explain by association and analogy. He isn't above either paradox or erudite digression. The actor listens as though carved out of stone: so far nothing the director has said has made any impact on him or helped clarify his character or role. One day a seasoned Polish actor interrupted his director's long, rambling monologue to ask, pointing to his fellow actor: "All that's well and good. But all I really want to know is: do I like this guy or not?"

There have been times when I've been involved with ambitious actors who are convinced the role they are playing now is what will decide their future. They made superhuman efforts to capture the essence of their character, convinced that only by so doing would they succeed in their allotted task. The problem is, such a sense of responsibility paralyzes an actor. No real emotion can circulate freely in bodies transfixed with fear. What is more, their faces are frozen, unable to convey nuances of expression. Bathed in a cold sweat, impressed beyond belief that they have had the great good fortune to be playing in this very important film, they are blind to the individual emotions they ought to portray. Actors such as these are constantly dissatisfied with themselves, and focus all their energies and attention on the text: they make up new dialogues, concoct new scenes, spend hours trying on costumes, meddle in everything—in short, do everything but concentrate on the character they are supposed to be portraying. It's not an easy illness to cure. As for myself, I always try to separate the actor per se from the role he is playing. I explain to him that there is no point in trying to make oneself resemble the character, physically or spiritually, that artifice is the key to the acting profession, and that there is nothing to gain in trying to identify existentially with the character one is "playing." The director has no choice but to explain as clearly as possible what he expects from an actor, and to control his acting as carefully and shrewdly as possible. If that doesn't work the director should get rid of him right at the start of shooting.

12

Test Shots
Are Indispensable

The usefulness of test shots is not limited to casting. They can answer all kinds of questions about your upcoming film: how do the dialogues sound on screen? What do the costumes look like on film? How is the crew performing?

These test shots can have a determining influence on the film. You should take them as seriously as you take the actual shooting, not as gratuitous or of secondary importance. Every film is a challenge. The test shots can help you clarify the focus of the subject, the script, and the actual film-to-be.

I prefer not to separate the technical test shots of the cameraman from the tests of the actors themselves. The notion that the actors' screen tests should be "objective" or "neutral" is wrong. I want to see the actors on-screen dressed in the costumes they'll be wearing, with the same kind of lighting we'll use for the real shooting. I generally try to make sure these test shots are done not in the studio but outside, usually on locations we plan to use for the film. Shooting in the open gives us a better sense of reality—the actor's face does not appear, as it would in the studio, as though emerging from some conventional shadow, but acquires an objective existence—as do the sky, the trees, or the snow on the site where you're shooting.

This is also the final stage during which the chief cameraman, or director of photography, "depicts" the future film to reassure the director. Here we are faced with reality: will the cameraman be able to transmute this strange, incongruous, and problematic world into a meaningful whole on screen? Will the actors, surprised at having to perform outdoors, suddenly forget their favorite tricks and perform more naturally when faced with the truth of the natural world around them?

Most of the time producers feel this phase of filmmaking is a waste of time and money, a whim on the part of the director. The crew often considers it a necessary evil preceding the "real work." In my experience, the test-shooting phase of the picture, assuming it is done properly, can save the future film from failure: at least it will have spared me from unnecessary surprises.

Here are a few practical suggestions:

1. Never let the actor learn his lines by heart for a test shot. Make up all kinds of excuses, blame it all on your assistant directors, do whatever you have to do, but under no circumstances give him the text till the very last minute, when the camera is ready to roll. This way you will learn whether or not the actor really understands the meaning of the scene. If he does, he will improvise to good effect.

2. Have the camera accompany the character's movements instead of creating unnecessary difficulties by complicated or fancy shots. I have always found that long shots are the best, since they intrude the least on the actor's movements and allow him to act as he would like, without interference. The long shot is also the only way the director can observe the actor carefully later on in the projection room. Test shooting requires patience and an open mind. If after one attempt I come up with an idea I think would be better, I tell the actor and we shoot it again. By the same token, actors may also come up with their own ideas of how a scene should be shot differently, and in that case I inevitably oblige.

Test shots, or camera tests as they are sometimes called, are not simply for the purpose of casting. It also gives the director an opportunity to see the proposed actors performing, which helps eliminate all kinds of misunderstandings and problems that inevitably arise in the first week of shooting. I think for instance of Daniel Olbrychski, the star of *Landscape after Battle*: during the camera tests he was made up and dressed as he would be in the film. That, plus the fact we shot outdoors, enabled him to create the character of the hero of the film well before the shooting began.

You should also try to avoid giving screen tests to too many actors—and above all, to too many actresses—in the vain hope that if you broaden your net you're sure to catch the right fish. In a meat market like that, no one can give his best. It just drains them of all self-confidence. What too often happens is that each new candidate at the try-out ends up mimicking those who have preceded him, after which everything turns shades of gray. On the contrary, screen tests should give the actors the feeling that the tests are simply to confirm a choice you've already made.

Another key piece of advice: never turn your camera tests over to assistant directors. What you would see on-screen would obviously be something you have not witnessed personally. You would therefore be missing the one thing that is essential, namely, your own immediate reaction to what you witnessed during the shooting, what you liked and what you didn't like. You can only get that kind of response from direct personal contact.

The first time I met Krystyna Janda was during the screen tests for *Man of Marble*. What struck me especially was the way she was smoking her cigarette while the camera was being prepared and the lighting set up. I had never seen such nervous intensity in my life. I was fascinated, and later I remarked to her that I thought she should try to recapture that intensity in the screen test itself. And she did, with such perfection and precision that

42

I knew right away I was dealing with an actress who was fully aware of what she was doing, a consummate artist and not one of those actresses who, under similar circumstances would ask, "Tell me, what did you like about what I just did?"

I have already mentioned my first encounter with Jerzy Radziwillowicz, long before I had selected him for the role in *Man of Marble*, at the Warsaw Drama School. All the screen did was confirm my choice. His smile, his utterly natural way of speaking, the innocence of his improvised speeches, convinced me on the spot that I had found someone unique. In fact, those screen tests were so good that we ultimately incorporated one of them into the final film.

During the past few years these camera tests have more often than not been shot on videotape, and I have also resorted to the video camera in this area. The film *Without Anesthesia* was to be shot entirely in one apartment. I took advantage of this situation of a single location to videotape the entire film, using the actors I had already had in mind when I was writing the script. Obviously in doing this it was not a matter of choosing the cast but rather of getting a bird's-eye view of the entire film. The results were utterly discouraging. So much so that I contemplated not doing the film at all. I had a similarly discouraging experience with the same medium when I made a videotape of a group of actors in preparation for the film version of *Danton*.

I attribute these experiences to the fact that, for a director who has grown up with and been formed by film, video is a technique that offers no resistance. The lighting is always sufficient, the camera movement incredibly light and facile—too facile—and what is more, if you don't like what you just did you can simply erase it and start again from scratch, which means the possibilities are infinite. This means you work without tension, without the familiar atmosphere of being on the edge, constantly at risk. The problem, of course, is that that tension, that sense of risk, is precisely what characterizes the work in a good film. And you should sense that same tension during your camera tests.

Needless to say, there is another way to cast your film, and that is to resort to agency files and film catalogs. But this process has always reminded me of those arranged marriages that emanate from the public announcements or dating services: the elements involved are despair on the one hand and cynicism on the other. I know that in countries where the "marketplace" of potential actors is enormous, directors often have to resort to this means of casting their films, but I could never feel confident about it. For me, it would at best be a first step in the casting process.

13

The
Production Schedule
Is Also Part of Directing

Let's take a close look at the production schedule. It charts the whole complicated process involved in making the film, indicating the days, the weeks, and the months (days off marked in color!). The calendar begins with the first day of shooting and ends on the last. The preshooting portion, and the postshooting work—the editing and sound mixing—are not part of the production schedule. How much time those two take depends on a number of circumstances, but the shooting schedule, which is the most costly part of filmmaking, demands scrupulous preparation. The production schedule lays out, for crew and cast alike, who will be doing what and when they will do it. The left-hand column contains the names of the characters and the actors who will play them. With a good production schedule you can see at a glance everything you need to know. Naturally, a schedule like this cannot be drawn up without a detailed knowledge of the shooting script.

Each scene (in fact, each action that takes place without interruption at the same location) has its own call sheet, which comprises:

- The main characters
- The secondary parts
- The number of walk-on parts
- The necessary props
- The special effects
- Any special equipment such as cranes or supplementary lighting that the crew might not typically have on hand

All the scenes shot on the same location will be filmed together. It would be too costly to shoot the film chronologically, that is, to come back to the same location several times. We call this method shooting in sequence. On the production schedule these "sequences" will appear in vertical columns, which indicate which actors are needed at which point.

The production schedule also has the virtue of showing the director and his assistants at a glance exactly what has been done and what remains to be shot, which actors have completed a given role, and which have not yet begun, where and what the crew are doing at any given moment (any production schedule includes those periods when no shooting is being done, when the crew is setting up at a new location). The production schedule gives you a picture of the entire film, making it easier to maintain control over it.

The order in which a film is shot depends on a number of factors: structural, atmospheric, financial, and technical. Believe me, the conception and preparation of a shooting schedule require as much inspiration and imagination as any other creative endeavor. If you fail to recognize the artistic considerations involved in putting together a production schedule, you risk jeopardizing your picture before it starts. That is why the Association of Polish Filmmakers grants production assistants the status of artists.

Almost every picture made includes outdoor scenes and the

script carefully notes the season when each scene takes place. It is vital that the script indicate the seasons, especially for a film that moves in time from one season to another, from one year to the next. To show the passage of time on the screen we alternate scenes set in different seasons: one shot in the countryside in summer, with shimmering heat and bright sunshine, followed by a shot of city roofs covered with snow. One doesn't need words to tell an audience that a certain period of time has passed. The passage of time, therefore, is a key element of the production schedule: most films take from ten to twelve weeks to shoot, and if there is a change of season or seasons you have to figure out in which time period your shooting should start. If you're moving from summer to winter, you may still want to start your winter scenes first, and then hope that by late spring you can create the illusion of summer on-screen. Of course if money is no concern, you can always move your cast and crew to a country or place where the climate you need is available.

One slight error in the production schedule can result in chaos: delays, complications, having to shoot in a studio scenes you planned to shoot outdoors, perhaps even having to construct studio landscapes. All of this can easily lead to financial as well as artistic disaster.

14

Shooting:
Begin with the Essential,
Finish with the Secondary

Every film is unique, it's true, but certain things are common to all. If you don't want to get bogged down and lose your way, don't begin shooting the flashes, the scenes of secondary importance. Some young directors think that by doing so the actors will have a chance to "warm up," to get in shape for the major scenes to come. Nothing could be further from the truth. An actor who begins with transitional or secondary scenes will not be able to settle seriously into his role. Take for example the direction "He walks down the street." Fine. But where is he coming from? Where is he headed? What is he feeling? Only the scenes that precede and follow this flash can tell us. Let's take a mundane example. Your character is leaving his mistress's apartment and is on his way home to his wife. Now picture the opposite situation. In each instance the man would be walking differently, thinking different thoughts, feeling different emotions . . . all of which the actor has to convey. In fact, only an actor who has already played the preceding crucial scene could convey that difference, especially when he is portrayed in a long shot.

If you start by shooting the secondary scenes, you'll not only be wasting your film but also the energy of your crew, which in the early stages of shooting is inevitably higher than it will be later on. Because of that heightened energy, you'll find you and your crew spending too much time on details that don't matter. Much of this secondary material will probably end up on the cutting room floor anyway, so why spend so much time on it? To get the best results during the first days of shooting, so that the crew jells together and gets enthusiastic about the film, begin by shooting the most important scenes, the ones that clarify and illustrate the basic premise of the picture. This way the actors will be able to understand their characters more profoundly, and the director will be immediately able to indicate his vision of the picture.

As for the final scene, when should it be shot? Every film closes with a shot that is intended to be memorable. It's a scene that requires special effort and care. You can't always get the desired effect on the first attempt; you often have to shoot it a number of times to get it just right. You should avoid leaving it to the end of the shooting itself. It's better to shoot it somewhere around the middle of the filming, when the crew is still up and the director already has a total picture of the film. I have never succeeded in maintaining the same tension with the crew from beginning to end of a film. The last days of shooting are usually mediocre. You tend to rush things and the initial enthusiasm has waned. Under these conditions, it would be better not to shoot as crucial a scene as the final one in the film.

15

The Set Decorator Is Not
an Imitator

The set director for *All the President's Men* won an Oscar for his
representation of the newsroom of *The Washington Post*, a set
so realistic you had the feeling the film had to have been shot
at the newspaper offices themselves. Filmmakers who should have
known better expressed surprise that set decorator George Gaines
should have been thus rewarded, for at best wasn't an imitator
being rewarded and not a creator? To answer that question fairly,
let us try to take a look at the role of the set decorator in an era
when most films are indeed shot in authentic exteriors or interiors.

In principle, the set decorator's first job is to find the best
locations. He adapts them, changes them, makes them work in
concert with the action of the film, and acts as the director's
guide. "In this scene the camera goes here. In that one you need
to hide it." Actually it's not usually all that simple. There are
times when what we are seeing with our own eyes cannot be
transferred to the screen. There are surroundings that just can't
be photographed. I know that the set of *All the President's Men*
looked just like the newsroom of *The Washington Post*. But we
also know it couldn't have been, if only because if the film had

really been shot there, the newsroom would have been out of service for several weeks . . . and the paper probably out of business. But there's another very good reason why this set had to be re-created in a studio. If the film had been shot in the real newsroom, we never would have been able to get a sense of the whole space, since part of it would always have been taken up with the camera and equipment. In a studio, however, the equipment could be located outside the set itself, thus offering a complete view of the office. Movable partitions could also be used to good advantage. And finally (this is of crucial importance) the set decorator could, under studio conditions, select and utilize the significant elements of the newsroom to create a density and meaning that he could not have obtained by using the real newsroom.

It is obvious that such a decision—to re-create the newsroom under studio conditions—was very costly and could perhaps be fully appreciated only by specialists. But the director must also take into account the restrictions and difficulties of shooting in an existing interior. Take the light for instance: the sun inevitably follows its prescribed course every day, but as it does, the light changes and thus reduces the amount of time a crew can work, unless the decision is made to black out the windows and use artificial light. But in so doing you lose one of the most precious elements of shooting in actual settings: the view out the windows of the house or apartment and authentic daylight. Of course, artificial lighting has its own limitations: the only place you can place your lamps is on the ceiling, which remains invisible, or else you have to hide them in corners, and that doesn't always create the right illusion. Thus when we're shooting in real interiors, we try to find places with a balcony where we can set up the lights, or else shoot on the ground floor where the lamps, placed on movable scaffolding, reinforce or replace the sun's light.

The conclusion is obvious. The poor use real settings in making their films, whereas millionaires can allow themselves the luxury of creating their settings in studios where it is far easier to work. We unlucky devils are reduced to intensifying the illusion of truth in natural settings, to seize from real life the slightest lighting effect in order to re-create the fleeting experience.

The success of the set is also dependent upon the lighting technique and the work of the cameraman. This dependence demands from the set decorator a profound knowledge of cinematic art. He must know not only how to read a script intelligently, but also how to assess it financially. An architect and plastic artist at first, he will become a cinema lover and cinema maker. Always on the lookout for new locations, he will photograph whatever strikes his fancy. He will collect and file forever in his mind the richness of the visual world in order to be able to pass on that knowledge and information to the director, who in turn will know how to put it to good use. No, the set decorator is not an imitator—he is trying to master the unattainable art, to reinstate nature by artificial means.

Over the past ten years or so I have only twice worked under studio conditions, with sets that were built specifically for my films. All my other films were shot in existing interiors. That says a great deal about the evolution of the role of the set decorator.

It's easy and pleasant to work in a studio. Your fitting rooms and prop storage rooms are right there. The light outside the windows doesn't change. And yet I would turn my back on a studio without a moment's hesitation if I had the opportunity of shooting my film in a real apartment, a real office, a real factory. The restrictions that those real settings imply automatically encourage the director to become more creative, the director of photography to look for new solutions to lighting problems. An

52

authentic interior gives me the reassuring feeling of being in a place that bears the stamp of real life. It's a place linked organically to the world around it: the elevator, the stairway, the courtyard, the door into the building, the street outside. And above all, such a place tells us something about the life of the people who live there.

The choice of locations for different sequences will be dictated by two kinds of considerations: does the setting fulfill the requirements of the script and the director's vision of the film? Does it add to the visual enrichment of the film? On the other hand, is the choice compatible with the crew's production schedule, in terms of distance and access and so on?

All these pros and cons have to be weighed very carefully before a final decision about any given location is made; both artistic and practical demands have to be taken into account, especially in these days when the shooting schedule for most pictures is no more than five to seven weeks, and where any time taken to move from one location to another can have a negative effect on the time allotted for shooting itself. The task of scouting out possible locations is initially given to the assistant directors, who then present their findings to the director. In my experience, assistant directors are an ambitious lot, ready to go to the ends of the earth in search of the perfect spot. For the sake of the production, it is a good idea to cool their ardor. The best way is to ask them to confine themselves to locations within walking or cycling distance.

If the set decorator wants to make himself really useful to the director, he has to renounce his original profession, which is that of builder of imaginary spaces, and turn himself into a tramp, someone who walks endlessly, who by his behavior and demeanor will be admitted to the most unexpected places, who will be able to sneak in unobserved to the nooks and crannies of private homes and offices alike, sizing up everything solely in terms of the film to be made. He will take Polaroids, make sketches and working drawings on paper tablecloths and old envelopes, to show the director later.

Another of his tasks is to be completely familiar with films past, to know when he sees an ideal location whether or not another filmmaker has already been there. If he uses a location that has been filmed before, then it is the set decorator's job to make it new by changing a door here, covering up a window there, repainting a wall or two. He will also know at what time the light is best at any given location and whether the noise of the streetcar will interfere with the sound recording. Today the set decorator is closer to a filmmaker than he is to a graphic artist. Thus my friend Allan Starski, who could have constructed a beautiful manor house in a studio, convinced me to film *The Young Ladies from Wilko* in a decaying and decrepit country house about fifty kilometers from Warsaw, for the sole reason that one could *feel* the lives of those who had been there, and that would have been impossible to re-create under studio conditions.

Can one judge the set of any film by the degree to which by sleight of hand it succeeds in imitating nature? There are scarcely any films in which the open sky does not have a part, but there is no way to imitate the truth of the sky. That is the landmark of all cinema. Laurence Olivier's film version of *Henry* V (1944) is exceptionally beautiful and scenically coherent, but its stylization breaks down as soon as we move to the battle scenes at Agincourt. Some directors, aware of this danger, flatly eliminate the "false note": the whole film is shot in the studio, including the trompe l'oeil sky. But in my view these films suffer from a frozen uniformity that makes them boring. Nothing will ever replace the original screen of the heavenly vault above our heads!

The set decorator who imitates life in films is indeed an artist.

16

Costumes or Clothes?

For the vast majority of contemporary films, it is hard to decide what the actors should wear. They often act in their own clothes. Under such circumstances, what is the role of the costume designer?

The following anecdote is a good illustration of the problem and situation. On the first day of shooting *Ashes and Diamonds*, Zbyszek Cybulski arrived at seven in the morning and went directly to wardrobe. Shortly thereafter I saw him reappear walking swiftly and purposefully, followed closely by two dressers who were shouting with despair: "Mr. Wajda! Mr. Wajda! He doesn't want to change his clothes!"

Zbyszek was dressed in the same "costume" I had known him to wear throughout the many years we had been friends: blue jeans, a green military jacket, a knapsack of rough fabric slung across his shoulder, and boots. After having tried on all the various costumes that had been prepared for him, he had decided that the clothes he was wearing were a better "costume" than any other he had seen. He was himself, and he wanted to give to the film the best of himself, his own integrity, right down to his boots and the metal canteen sticking out of his knapsack.

Here's another example, this time from *Promised Lands*. We had hundreds of extras to dress for this film, and instead of trying to make or order costumes for them, we went through some clothing warehouses and improvised. Sometimes certain combinations of clothing were so striking that we eventually used them for the main characters. In other words, by combining ready-made clothes and our own imaginations, we came up with costumes that were more authentic and varied than if we had had them made from scratch. Of course, we wouldn't have got the same results if I had not spent countless hours myself in the clothing warehouse, and then countless more with the actors and extras trying on what we had concocted.

Costumes can serve as a support to actors, but they can also have a negative effect. Try, for example, to get a young, handsome actor to wear trousers that are too big for him. If he's a talented professional he will see, after a moment's hesitation, that these oversized trousers are one indication of how the director sees him in the role. If he's not so sharp, he will probably perform beneath his ability, or beneath the performance he would have given with a neutral costume. Knowing how to advise an actor about what clothes he or she should wear in a film is as important a talent for a costume designer as are the sketches and sense of color.

One of my friends, the particularly gifted costume designer Jerzy Szeski, used to pick some costume that he was especially proud of and put it on himself. Then he would wear it on the set until it finally caught my eye and I realized that he had come up with a new marvel that he wanted me to assign to one of the actors.

Finally, one important practical piece of advice: avoid if at all possible this maniacal habit of having actors change costumes for every scene. The costume designer will make a point of telling you that a new costume (actually, a new jacket, for trousers barely count and shoes are rarely visible on screen) will help actors give better performances. That may well be, but when the director arrives at the editing process and for whatever reason has to modify the order of various scenes in the film—which is commonplace, and almost inevitable—this fastidiousness on the part of the costume designer can make the editing process a nightmare. A jacket change, even a new tie, can be the obstacle to improving the film in the editing process.

17

A Group of Friends
Make a Film

Always together, laden down with heavy equipment, a film crew reminds me of a commando team or a band of snipers. The only problem is, unlike their military equivalents, the film crew has had no schooling together.

In my view there are only three ways to put together a good film crew:

1. You may have the good fortune to inherit the crew of some important director who is between two pictures. But the problem here is that such a crew will inevitably compare everything you do with what their own director would do under similar circumstances. If you do the same things he does, you've lost your individuality. If you try to win over the affections of such a crew, you'll inevitably fail, for their loyalties lie elsewhere. For a young director, this is the worst of all possible choices.

2. When I was preparing my first film, *Generation*, I gathered around me a group of friends when I was still writing the script. They were all still amateurs, but they had staked everything on the film and on me. If your film is original, that is, breaks new ground or tries to venture into realms unknown cinematically, then you're going to need fresh people: a director of photography

who, faced with tough technical problems, will be able to come up with competent technical solutions; and a sound engineer who will be able to adapt what he learned at school to your particular needs. I suspect that the vast majority of new techniques available to us today have come from such novices, slightly mad, without much experience, but also without the mind-set that some hardened professionals bring to the set. I had the great good fortune to begin my career with such a crew.

3. There is a third method, the simplest: hire topnotch professionals and pay them handsomely, a crew who can handle any situation. As Polonius said to the actors who came to Elsinore, "Seneca cannot be too heavy, nor Plautus too light." I am told that such crews do exist. The director Roman Polanski once told me that the only reason he ever went to Hollywood was because it was the place where you could find these professionals. That may well be. As for myself, I would much prefer to rob a bank with a gang of rank amateurs than be part of a group of professional gangsters.

Whether you like it or not, you must become friends with the crew, and that means with everyone, not just the director of photography and the set decorator and the costume designer but also the crane operator and the grip.

It's not something you learn to do overnight, but it's something that comes naturally as you grow professionally. As soon as you start, as an assistant director, say, you should spend as much time as your duties allow cultivating the other members of the crew, gaining their confidence and winning their friendship. Later on, when you become a director yourself, those friendships will serve you in good stead.

A film crew made up of friends represents to my mind an appreciable advantage over any other arrangement. You should of course be aware that with such a crew you, the director, will receive more than your share of friendly advice. Some directors make it clear from the outset of shooting that they will listen to no advice. I suspect that such people are afraid of having to share their fame (or perhaps their fortune) with someone else. My advice to such directors is that if you are strong-minded and purposeful, no one can make you change your mind anyway. And if, on the contrary, you have an open mind, why not listen to advice that might be helpful? Napoleon used to say that battle plans were doubtless the result of a collective effort, but all that really counted was the person who carried them out, for he was the one who assumed the full responsibility. In our case, the director will always have to assume the final responsibility.

Before you begin shooting, give your script to a number of trusted friends. As the time for the actual shooting approaches, you will probably listen too carefully to their comments and criticisms of the script. But the secret of the film resides within yourself. The script is only the tip of the iceberg, the bulk of which is submerged in the sea of your imagination. If you remain faithful to your own vision of the film, you should have no fear of listening to and culling from the ideas and advice that your friends proffer. Once on-screen, those ideas will belong to you and you alone.

18

Our Film—My Film

"My film," "my script," "the script adapted from my original idea" are statements I have heard directors say over and over again. In the course of shooting any film, however, I strongly suggest that you downplay the "I" and emphasize the collective "we." To ensure the film's success you need the collaboration and unity of the whole crew. I will go even further and add that if the film is a success, even if you go on referring to it as "our film," the audience and reviewers will still think of it as the director's. If it's a flop, however, you will have to assume full responsibility: it will become again "my film" whether you like it or not.

Many years ago I made a film about the last cavalry squadron to hold out against the Germans in the Polish–German war of 1939. It was called *Lotna*, which was the name of one of the mares in the squadron. A fews days after it opened, I gathered up all the newspapers and read them one after the other, seated by myself on a bench in the park. They were overwhelmingly bad. After the success of my first films—*Kanal* and *Ashes and Diamonds*—it was a rude awakening, all the more so because I was aware that I had committed every possible error in the making

61

of this film. In fact, there was something about this film that made it stand out from the others. There was something special about it, something that set it apart from the films that had enjoyed success and been uniformly admired. I began to wonder whether my errors did not emanate from my originality, whereas my virtues were perhaps nothing more than a certain professional knowledge and ability that I shared with lots of other filmmakers. That realization did not make *Lotna* a better film, but that moment of reflection and lucidity led me to ask these crucial questions: "What do I like?" "What do I know how to do?" "What would I like to see on the screen?"

For years now I've been reworking *Lotna* in my mind, improving and correcting it, completing it. It's the only picture I would like to do over again. I love this stepchild of mine: it will remain forever "my film."

19

Some of the Most Frequent Misunderstandings

All some young ladies have to do is cut their hair, don dark glasses and proclaim themselves "nihilists" for us to be convinced that wearing glasses carries with it personal convictions. . . . I also know some people who, having read a page that they barely understand, are immediately convinced that the ideas expressed are their ideas, sprung full-blown from their own mind.

—Fyodor Dostoyevsky

Every director in the world wants to do something original. Each of us tries to look at the world with our own eyes, but our task is made difficult because other, more original and talented artists have come before us and taken away some of the freshness of vision. One day I was flying from Palermo to Rome, thirty thousand feet up, when I saw through the plane window a sky that was bloodred and green: a mystical sunset. I was reveling in the joy of that moment of perfection when I realized that I had already seen that same sky, not from a plane but in a painting by Matthias Grünewald, his magnificent *Crucifixion*. Grünewald had, by the force of his imagination, somehow managed to rise above the clouds and depict a sunset that human eyes had never seen. That knowledge did not diminish my pleasure at the sunset I had witnessed from the plane, but it was no longer mine alone, no longer my discovery. In fact, if I experienced it with such intensity it was precisely because, without at first knowing it, I was remembering the Grünewald painting. It was he who had opened my eyes to the threatening combination of reds and greens.

After my first few films, the reviewers began to say that I was "a symbol-oriented director." Ever since then I have always been pursued by the white horse that appears in *Ashes and Diamonds*, the ineluctable sign of the Polishness of my films.

Each culture has its own symbols, but we should always remember that they neither depict the universal nor convey a single meaning. The black that we associate with mourning becomes white in Japan. For us white signifies innocence, purity, and virginity. Anyone who has ever directed *Hamlet* remembers the long scene in which the mad Ophelia hands out herbs that she has picked on the riverbank to the king, the queen, and Laertes. Their symbolism is well known and fully documented by Shakespearean scholars, but today's public has no knowledge of all this, with the sole exception of the plant called common rue, with its yellow flowers, which is linked to virginity (but even rue does not grow everywhere).

Some years ago one of our drama companies was invited to the city of Vilnius, in Lithuania, which has a significant Polish population. The play it put on was a romantic comedy by Juliusz Slowacki, which took place in a dilapidated Polish manor house that belonged to a count with the strange name of Fantazy. To inject a note of realism into the play, the director had rented some live chickens, which he placed in cages onstage. One of the chickens, terrified by the lights, managed to escape and hopped down into the orchestra pit, where it landed on the conductor's music stand, flapping its wings. The chicken was white, and the audience burst into spontaneous applause: to the public the director was using that white bird to symbolize Poland's national emblem, a white eagle.

"That's just what I wanted," or "Don't you see that I did that on purpose?" you will often hear the young or relatively inexperienced director say in response to attacks or negative comments about his film. That automatic defense mechanism would seem to be justified—any artist has the right to his own vision as well

64

Andrzej Wajda during the filming of *Ashes and Diamonds*.

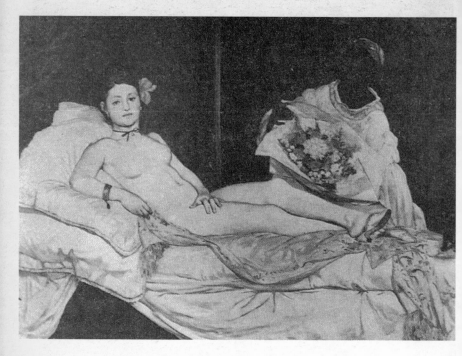

It isn't the nude, it's the portrait of a nude woman that upset the spectators. Edouard Manet, *Olympia*, 1863 (Louvre Museum).

Zbigniew Cybulski, on the first day of filming *Ashes and Diamonds*. ▶

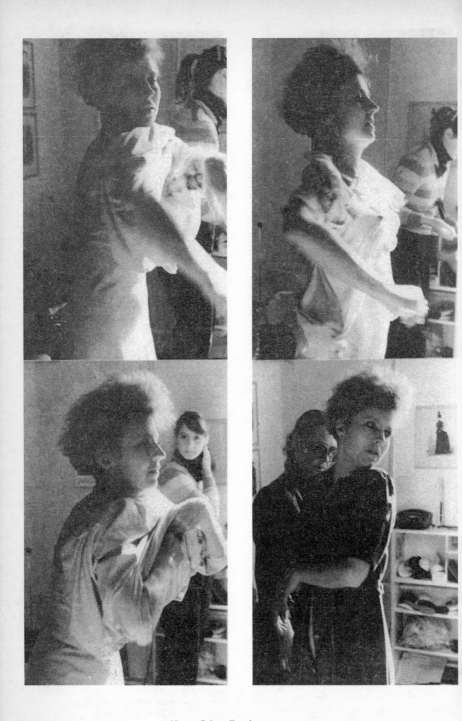

Hanna Schygulla tries on costumes.

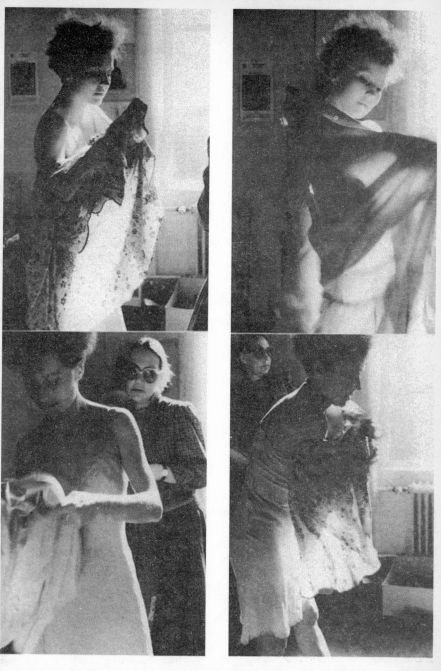

This light and shadow effect, obtained quite by chance in these photos, would be recaptured in the lighting of *A Love in Germany* by cameraman Igor Luther.

To perform in front of the camera – that's acting!
Krystyna Janda and Jerzy Radziwillowicz in *Man of Marble*.

Daniel Olbrychski created the main character of *Landscape After the Battle* long before filming began, during the test shots.

Lotna (1958): storyboards of the final scene

My mistakes are perhaps more characteristic than my virtues.

The death of Marat: drawing and painting by Jacques Louis David.

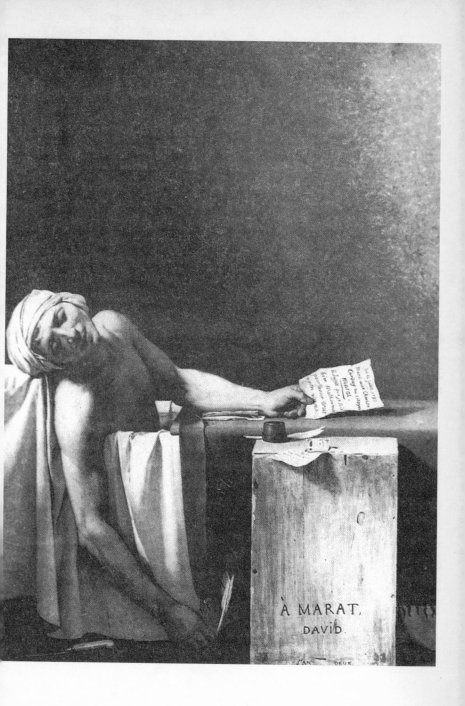

The vertical format of the painting is arbitrary — and essential.

You will stop in front of this painting at the exact distance Rembrandt intended.
The Sampling Officials at the Cloth-makers Guild, Rijksmuseum, Amsterdam.

Don't forget proper lighting for the eyes!

Gerard Depardieu and Wojtek Pszoniak in *Danton*.

Sir John Gielgud in *The Orchestra Conductor*.

The master (in black) and the assistant (in white), faithful shadow of the
director. Photo taken during the filming of Tadeusz Kantor's *The Dead C*

Andrzej Wajda in conversation with Lech Walesa during the strike at the
Lenin shipyard in Gdansk, August 1980.

Cinematic Group X in February 1982, shortly before it was forcibly dissolved.

as the right to defend that vision. Yet the public may agree with the premise of the film or it may not. It may accept the director's vision of the world and humanity, or it may not. But one thing is certain: it is the director's job to make sure the audience can always follow the thread of the action. In my experience, most of the misunderstandings that arise between the public and the director derive precisely from the filmmaker's tendency to mistake the weaknesses in his film for originality. Any imprecision in the plot or action relates to the "mystery" of his work. That is why I advise the young director never to resort to "That's just what I wanted"—for in the cinema the only judge is the public. You'll realize the truth of that statement the first time you have a successful picture and see long lines waiting to see it.

This indissoluble link between the picture and its public is in the final analysis essential. In all his films Charlie Chaplin concocted the most unbelievable situations, but they were grounded in the kinds of hopes and dreams we all have and understand. Who would not love to come upon a nugget of gold (*The Gold Rush*)? Who would not hate working on a robotized assembly line in a factory (*Modern Times*)? How many men have dreamed of having at least three wives (*Monsieur Verdoux*)? Chaplin never strayed very far from these basic hopes and illusions. He was a beloved figure from one end of the world to the other, despite the fact that his films always ended up showing how these dreams and hopes were unattainable. Chaplin knew that however difficult life was, man was an inveterate dreamer who always believed that a better life was just around the corner, even if it meant battling with a grizzly bear, standing up to a straw boss, or risking your neck on the guillotine.

For us directors, Chaplin is the consummate artist of our profession, the best example of what a filmmaker can aspire to. I always remember the stories about Chaplin sending his assistant directors into the suburbs with reels of film fresh out of the camera, after which he would anxiously ask: "Did the children laugh?"

20

On the Set

For the occasional observer chancing upon a film crew in the process of shooting, I'm sure the impression is one of a group of crazies completely out of control. And despite all the years I've been in the business, I must confess that when I step back and observe what is happening on any given day on the set I have the same feeling of absurdity. Each film is special, unique in itself, which explains that no matter what you've learned in the past you can be sure in any new venture you'll have your fair share of new and unanticipated surprises. Despite all this, I'll do my best to describe how I work on the set.

I begin my working day during the shooting by rehearsing the actors. The previous evening I discuss the scene with the actors, the director of photography, and the assistant directors, both as to its place in the film and what we want to accomplish from it. Now, the following morning, we need to work out the mechanics on the site itself, which has been meticulously prepared before we arrive.

I show the actors where each of them will be placed and then slowly and carefully work through the entire scene with them, from beginning to end. That gives me a sense of how it works as a totality, the rhythm of the scene (is it too slow, too fast?), and to see how the actors are performing and interacting.

During this on-set rehearsal the director of photography is also hard at work. He too is seeing how the actors are performing, while at the same time listening to what the director is saying and indicating in sign language where the lights should go and what camera angle or angles he wants. The whole scene will not, of course, be shot in one take, but a good portion of it will be done in a master shot that will give us a good overall view of the actors' performance, singly and collectively, which can be viewed on-screen. This will generally be a long shot so that we can see the full view of all the actors. But we resort to medium shots and close-ups if necessary, and try out zooms and other techniques if we plan to use them or want to test something.

If the cinema—as many people today believe—consists first and foremost of photographing movement, if the camera is indeed the main character of the picture, that ought to be our starting point. That at least seems to be the opinion of a great number of younger directors.

This is more or less how they work on the set: the director and the director of photography take turns looking into the view-finder, manipulating and monkeying with the camera as if this very special ballet were their principal preoccupation. Some-where along the way they manage to frame the actors and actresses in their viewfinder, only to see that *they*—the director and camera crew—are being watched with detachment by the actors. Finally they have to knuckle down to the reality of filming these people, who are already showing signs of boredom. At this point, there is no easier way to make sure the actors are discouraged than by starting with an important scene and expecting them to shine. The danger, of course, is that a film made like this is not in any condition to *tell* anything whatsoever. It ends up being a "show," with the director in the role of assistant cameraman, and both he and the cameraman befuddled by their preoccupation with "interesting" angles.

If, when I shot the scene of Cybulski's death in *Ashes and Diamonds*, which takes place on a garbage heap, I had placed the camera too close to his face, the audience would never have seen the convulsions of his legs, whereas by making it a medium-long shot we see him all curled up, in a fetal position, as he expires. That scene exists on the screen because the camera was admiring him while he, the consummate actor, was completely indifferent to it.

Let's come back to the master shot, which will have given us an overview of the whole scene. Now what I do is move in closer and film the scene from a number of different angles, which allows me to grasp the scene through its various fragments. At this point I will have a clear idea of which shots I want to do in close-up. This procedure may lead one to believe that the director is at the mercy of both the actors and the camera techniques. That may well be, but real freedom is not won by doing away with structure and discipline. That structure can be destroyed by the traditional director as well as by the most radical newcomer. No matter how much advance work you may have done in preparing the scene, no matter how meticulously you may have run through it and prepared your camera angles, the actual shooting may well produce all sorts of unexpected and unanticipated surprises. The only difference is that with all that preparation the director will be conscious of what is happening at all times. No quirk of fate will take him completely by surprise, nor will there be any negative results because he hesitated for a moment.

How do you convey action in a film? Let's imagine for a moment a football or soccer stadium, where a match is being covered for television. In order for the television audience to be able to follow the match, all the cameras are lined up on one side of the stadium, as though the action were taking place on a stage. The spectator will always know which is his team's goal, and which the opponent's, and thus be able to follow the course of the match up and down the field. What would happen if some crazy director placed one of the cameras on the other side of the stadium, so that when that camera was cut in the spectator suddenly saw the ball going in the opposite direction from the way all the other cameras had oriented his thinking?

Is there an analogy between that situation and a feature film? Perhaps not, but some directors consciously make their films in such a way that we lose all sure sense of time and place. There is always a danger here that unless such ambiguity is created by a major artist, the audience can quickly lose all sense of what is going on and lose interest.

Once you have completed the master shot, and the various angled close-ups, the time is ripe to focus all your attention on the actors. I remember those times when we all thought that actors gave their best performances during long shots: since the camera was always on them, we thought, it would record the finest nuances of their performance. No one thinks that way anymore.

Actually, that old method allowed actors to impose their own rhythms on the camera. Sometimes an actor reveling in his own magnificent performance would slow down the film, and the director would remain powerless to do anything about it. He couldn't even remedy the situation in the editing room, for the director will not have at his disposal any extra footage he can substitute or insert to make the film more dynamic. That style of directing still exists today, not in film, but in television dramas, where the economics are more stringent and the director does not have the time to shoot a scene in various segments and from different angles and distances. That is true in television for even the most complicated scenes.

My advice to actors getting ready to perform in front of a camera is that they should not try to impress the director by their profound and sophisticated knowledge of the character they are portraying. On the contrary, he should learn his part by successive stages, take the time and trouble to learn where he should be and how he should move. In rehearsing those key elements he'll repeat his part several times, even though he doesn't normally learn his part by heart at this stage. If he learns it too early he's likely to lose the freshness he'll bring to the part when at long last the director signals: CAMERA, ACTION!

Nevertheless, the first take is often not satisfactory. Even at the moment of maximum effort and concentration, the actor's attention will wander because of some unexpected technical detail. I generally repeat that initial take, and often shoot a third time if necessary. I don't think there's any point, however, in doing any more than that. In my experience ten retakes will not guarantee any better results, especially if you take into account all the time and effort that you have to spend on it. Even in those rare cases where I do several retakes of the same shot, I request that two or at most three are printed up, so that when we reach the editing process I won't be completely overwhelmed. On retakes I prefer to change the lens or move the camera slightly. That way I have the widest range of choices in the editing room.

The real difficulty in filmmaking, in my view, is making sure that throughout the picture there is a sense of continuity on all levels: the actors' performances, the atmosphere of each scene, the way they tie together, and the lighting. Only that basic sense of continuity allows the audience to follow the thread of the action from beginning to end. Without that continuity, the audience will essentially be dealing in bits and pieces that may in themselves be entertaining but which will not make sense from one scene to the other. Nothing is more difficult than creating this sense of continuity, for the director has to know precisely how the final product will look to the audience on the screen, and what will probably escape the audience's attention.

From the viewpoint of the actor, his hardest job is knowing, in every scene, exactly what the situation of his character is at that point. Unlike the stage, where the actor moves from an opening to a closing or climactic scene, films are always shot out of sequence. Unless the actor, therefore, is constantly aware of what has happened to his character prior to the scene being shot, what his state of mind is at this point, and what his relation to the other characters, it will be all too easy for him to lose himself in the seeming chaos. What is more, the actor must also constantly keep in mind the entire story, that is, be aware of his essential self in this nonchronological film world he has to deal with daily.

The best way to do this is simply for the actor to keep on asking himself some basic questions, as one often does in life:

- Who am I?
- Where have I come from?
- What do I know about what is happening here and now?
- What do I have to do to reach the goal imposed upon me by the denouement of this film?

If he doesn't keep asking himself this sort of question, there is a very good chance that the level of his performance will slip, or be inconsistent with what has preceded, and he will end up on the cutting-room floor. There is only one way to prevent this from happening: keep on creating the character at every moment. Think for a moment of the irresponsible director who, unhappy with James Dean's performance, edited out everything he found irritating about Dean's acting style. Don't worry: it never happened. That was merely to illustrate the point I was trying to make. There was no danger of that happening because James Dean was not simply original in particular scenes, at certain high points; his originality is evident in every single millimeter of the films he shot. But there we are dealing with that rarity, an actor of genius.

21

Film Sensitivity
and the Style of Photos

In the earlier days of filmmaking, the image you saw on the screen seemed to come from a camera placed outside the action and limited to recording and presenting "from without." That effect was the direct result of the weightiness and cumbersome nature of the cameras of the time.

The arrival of the light, portable camera, together with light-weight sound equipment and the arc light, completely changed the whole nature of film directing. Today the camera finds its place in the center of the action, where it can record in shots that are either very short or quite long or somewhere in between, thus creating a very rich mountain of graphic material for the director to work with in the editing process. In the editing room, too, the director can heighten many effects in a way he could never do before, to the point of eliminating altogether fades and transitional passages from one scene to another. In place of the beautiful, stately images of an earlier era, we have today a world that is fragmented and disintegrated, which in itself creates something dynamic and subjective. What this does is eliminate, or certainly lessen, the distinctions that used to exist between the performance of the actors, the composition of the image, the movement of the camera, the creative process of the editing. The result is a vital and stimulating cinema, which while different from the filmmaking of an earlier period still requires consummate professionalism and mastery of technique. In a sense, it is a cinema that derives from the life of large cities, with the staccato rhythm of their life, and their violence.

At the time I was making *Kanal*, we thought we were doing well if at the end of the day we had completed four to five takes. Today it is not unusual to come away at the end of a shooting day with as many as fifteen or twenty. This creates constant tension among the crew, because of the frenetic pace, but allows the director to move from one take to the next without losing the thread of the action while waiting for the camera and lights to be positioned.

Throughout the 1970s Polish filmmakers hoped and believed that the country was on the verge of becoming part of the contemporary world. They therefore seized upon this "new" style, hoping that the quickened pace of their films would somehow speed up the flow of blood through the veins of a worn-out social system. These films included Feliks Falks' *The Manipulator*, Krzysztof Zanussi's *Camouflage*, and my own *Man of Marble*.

Today any half-decent home video camera comes equipped with a zoom lens, which enables the user to move in on or away from the subject he is filming without moving the camera itself. The zoom video came into wide use when sports events began to be televised; with the flick of his finger a television technician could in the fraction of a second move you from a wide-angle view of the whole stadium or scene of action to a close-up so large that a football would fill the entire television screen—a very startling effect. It is precisely this movement of the camera which gives the illusion of depth and a sense of space. I would liken that use of the zoom lens to a dizzying descent onto a still photograph laid flat on some surface. The camera movement is here replaced by an optical process, as though we were seeing several still photographs superimposed one on top of the other. This gives the disconcerting impression that space has been "removed," which is in direct contradiction to our tendency to want to deepen the image. As a result it is not clear whether the zoom is really suitable for feature films, although that doesn't rule out its use by past, present, and future filmmakers.

Since I am not a film historian, I cannot say for sure who first used the zoom in an innovative way in feature films, but I believe it was the French director Claude Lelouche, in his 1966 film *A Man and a Woman*, in which he used the zoom lens with an ease and flexibility that had hitherto been unknown. This breakthrough showed others what was really possible. The movement of the traveling camera gives an illusion of space, whereas the zoom allows one to focus and move in on or away from the subject, allowing the director to choose precisely what will appear on the screen. There were also other "discoveries" of this kind. For example, you can cover the camera with an object that appears very close up and out of focus and then change the framing, removing the object to reveal a wide-angle view.

As a result of these new manipulations, we began to go in for very long takes. Faces and fragments of interiors began to float across the screen seconds before they appeared clearly in the shot itself. A number of short takes were spliced together to make a whole, creating an atmosphere of intense intimacy. A couple madly in love could thus melt into an animated street scene without any scenic preparation. The cameraman, hidden in some remote spot, invisible to the passing crowd, was at long last in a position to be able to follow the actors through the unpredictable and truthful world of the city. This was the great discovery of the 1970s, a discovery that still astonishes and moves us today: that we had the technical means to reflect and translate the multifaceted, unpredictable, constantly moving "chaos" of urban life.

Since then the cinema has reverted to some extent to tried-and-true techniques. Each scene is split up into an increasing number of individual takes. But out of this experience and these experiments one basic improvement has come: the director of photography and the camera crew are less and less occupied with the problem of lighting, and spend more of their time making the camera a creative instrument, imposing upon it their desired rhythm. Lighting and the use of the camera are one and the same—the work of the same artist.

22

The Director's Two Eyes

God blessed the film director with two eyes: one to watch the camera and one to take in everything going on around him. For the director this must become second nature, until the day he stops making films (and if you live in countries where political sensitivity is an issue in filmmaking, that day could come sooner than you expect. So don't waste any time!).

Lights, Camera, Action. Here is what the director has to be doing and observing simultaneously:

- The actors' performances.
- The movement of the camera and its synchronization with the action.
- What the crew is doing: are they paying close attention to the take? Will they be able to comment on it meaningfully later on?
- Is the lighting as it should be? (This is the lighting crew's job, of course, but the director must still check on it.)
- The sky: will the take be over before the clouds move in and cover the sun?
- Is the actor who is the focus of the camera's eye right now

going to knock over that priceless Chinese vase? And what about that microphone—isn't it dangerously low, so that you might be able to see it on-screen when you view the rushes?

And many, many more details of this kind.

All this may seem not just difficult but downright impossible, but think what it was like when you first learned to drive. When my friend Boleslaw Michalek, a film critic, bought his first car, he asked a friend of his to go with him to pick it up. Neither of them had any real driving experience, but Michalek decided that it would better if his friend drove. When they got in the car, the friend said in a quivering voice: "I'll concentrate on the motor. You keep your eyes on the road." Not far down the road they landed in a ditch.

In the early days of my career, I used to ask my assistant directors to keep their eyes on this or that during the shooting. But that led to all kinds of mishaps and misunderstandings and, in the course of the rushes, to real catastrophes.

No, the hard fact is that the director has to do all those things himself. And the crew has to know that everything it is doing is at every instant of the way controlled by the director, whose eye will not let anything pass. That's the only way to get impeccable results.

23

How to Film This Chatter, or: Dialogue On-Screen

For many filmgoers—and sometimes for me as well—movies today are reminiscent of a nonsensical old man who babbles on and on whether or not anyone is listening. Too many films today strike me as being overly wordy and overly long, works that are both self-indulgent and seemingly oblivious to the audience's own needs and demands. I know what I'm talking about since I'm aware of this destructive element in my own films. In its original incarnation, cinema was an art of the image, of ellipsis and action. It has become an art of chitchat and idle speech while at the same time the image, the pictorial quality—however beautiful and lovingly photographed—seems only remotely related to the text or the subject of the film, as though all too often the director was only interested in displaying his talent.

There is no doubt that film at the moment is dominated by dialogue. Our job, therefore, is to try and see what is the best way of filming this chatter, in order to retain a few healthy principles.

In the first place, scenes in which there is a great deal of talk should be rendered as "dynamic" as possible via movement, and this is especially true in those expository scenes that normally occur when you move from one key scene to another. The text apprises us of important facts we need to know to understand the course of the action; the places through which the characters pass will also help us understand where the plot is taking us next. There will come a point when the weary heroes will feel the need to sit down and talk things out. That, unfortunately, is inevitable, for if we film their faces as they are moving no one will be able to tell what they are thinking or what their deeper intentions are. When this point in the film comes, make sure you are paying close attention! Here you must shoot the scene so that nothing prevents the audience from focusing totally on the actors' facial expressions. When you speak to someone in real life you either look straight at him or you avert your gaze. Such details can indicate the meaning of the conversation, as much as the words themselves. All these things have to be translated to the screen, which isn't easy.

Here are three basic frames:

1. Two people speaking, seen more or less in profile
2. Close-ups of each of your two characters
3. Close-ups of the two characters with the arm of one of them just showing

The close-up of the speaker emphasizes the importance of what the actor is saying. His eyes, the mirrors of truth (or of lies), must be directed on the other character or averted, depending on what you want to get across. The question arises: where in relation to the camera lens are the eyes of the listener? And here we are, of course, not referring to the position of the actor to the left or the right of the camera lens, in other words, a profile shot.

The expression "withering gaze" clearly implies that the actor must know precisely where his adversary is. The latter is next to the camera. He speaks his lines, indicates his reactions—but that is not his "real" position. He is in fact standing in for the camera itself. His eyes are approximately at the level of the camera lens. This being the case, why can't the actor speaking look right at the lens? That would make everything so easy! The only problem is, that would reveal the existence of the camera. Think for a moment of all those streetside interviews where people's opinions are sought, or sports matches where the camera is focused right on the person being interviewed or on the crowd. Their automatic reaction is to wave and make faces and call out to their parents or friends. In both cases the presence of the camera is nakedly revealed. The actor, on the other hand, is not addressing the camera but his partner on the screen.

In a frame where we see two characters, the relation between their expressions is easy: either they look each other in the eye or they are avoiding each other's gaze, depending on the scene and the script. The difficulty arises when we cut the same dialogue up into two close-ups: now where is the person who is supposed to be listening? Next to the camera? Then how far away from the lens? Higher or lower? If the person speaking gets up and begins to move across the room, where should the actor who is speaking direct his gaze? How does that whole problem get resolved if both camera and crew are concealing the person being spoken to, whose responses emanate back to the actor on camera from somewhere back behind the camera?

In cases like this you have to trust your own visual memory by means of a mental editing process of two shots: the one you have just taken and the one you are doing right now. There is, and you will learn to know precisely where it is through experience and intuition, that perfect indefinable point where the gazes of the two characters should meet. It will be neither too high nor too low, too far nor too near: a point dictated by truth. Once this point has been found and made clear to the actors involved, it will enable them to interiorize the displacement between their gazes on the set and on the screen.

The actor delivering his lines manages to imagine the expression, the look, the movement of his off-screen partner. But he will never be able to act confidently until he knows where these elements are in relation to the camera. The look in a character's eyes and his gaze have a unique power of expression: one must do everything one can to keep that gaze from wandering or becoming expressionless.

24

Neither Too Near
nor Too Far

Every dialogue is made up not only of words but also of silent reactions to those words. The best way to make use of both aspects of dialogue is to shoot the scene with two cameras, each focused on one of the characters. This method is considered old-fashioned by many directors today, and contrary to their conception of the cinematic art. They are forgetting that the desired final effect can be obtained in the process of editing. Editing offers a director the opportunity to detect, from out of this mountain of filmed material, some tiny nuance of expression, some movement or expressive gesture, that will contribute to that desired effect.

The next time you are in Amsterdam, go spend some time looking at Rembrandt's 's masterpiece *The Sampling Officials at the Clothmakers Guild in Amsterdam*. I am sure that you will stop to look at the picture from precisely the distance Rembrandt wanted you to. The way the cloth merchants look at you out of the painting will make you go inevitably to that fixed point. In the painting the cloth merchants are gazing out expectantly, awaiting the arrival of someone else. Rembrandt got all his models to look toward that perfect point, the point at which the person arriving would appear. And, of course, that arriving cloth merchant is none other than you, the spectator who stops to look at this extraordinary painting.

I always try to place the camera in such a way that I have the best overall view of the actors' movements. There are exceptions to that rule, cases where it is necessary to depict on-screen some piece of architecture, a château, a long corridor, or the Eiffel Tower. In such cases, the camera has to be set up to be able to frame the subject in its entirety, so the audience can grasp in a second whether the scene is taking place in front of the Paris Opéra or in the door of a bank.

If you want to indicate a long corridor, place the camera at its entrance. That's the only way. If you want to shoot mountains, you will have to frame them from afar. If you try to shoot them by climbing the mountain, all you'll end up with on-screen is a bunch of rocks, which is not the soaring impression you wanted to convey. Shot from their base, mountains will seem small, unless there is a chain beyond, whose peaks are loftier than those in the foreground. The same holds true for the Eiffel Tower: you're doomed to failure if you try to photograph the monument by shooting its base. If you want to show it impressively, as though it were being seen for the first time, you should:

1. Photograph it from a distance. You can only get a real feeling of its size and immensity by depicting it in the context of the city.
2. Move up the camera and show a man at the base of the tower. This antlike creature can then be made to climb the tower, step by step up the endless staircase. Then you can show a second ascent, this time in the elevators.
3. The face of the man: the ant becomes spectator. By looking down from the top of the tower at Paris spread out beneath him, the man takes possession of what he sees and identifies himself with the Eiffel Tower's creator.

25

The Mystery:
In the Country
of Light and Shadow

Lighting is one of the most delicate realms of the cinematic art. How is it possible that shots taken under lighting conditions that are very different can give a beautiful and unified image? That is the secret of masters of the camera. But the director has to find out what that secret is, if only to control the director of photography's work and make sure it coincides with his own vision of the film.

Young directors tend to attach too much importance to that magic moment when, with one eye closed and the other glued to the viewfinder, they believe they are "controlling" what will appear on the screen. Guess again. A good part of what they are seeing through the viewfinder, in cooperation with the cameraman, will not be visible. What will be captured by the camera can be verified only by looking at the set. The best way of working is to check the framing of the first take and then the last, which will give you a fairly good idea of the dimensions of the scene. This way you will also be able to see how the lens will distort the actors' faces and the background.

In its aesthetic refinements, the cinema enjoys a very wide range of focal possibilities, from the extremely long (1,000, 500, 300, 250, 90, 75), to the extremely short (20, 18, 16, on down to 9.8), the very wide-angle lens called a Fish Eye, leaving the medium lenses (25, 35, 50) to be used for their old classic purposes. What are these many lenses for? Photography manuals will tell you that with a 500 lens you can capture the movement of a bird in flight, that with a lens in the 16–18 range you can photograph narrow interiors without problem. One should bear in mind that using too wide a variety of lenses in a film can detract from its sense of unity of style, suggesting the director may have wavered in his choice of lens from scene to scene. From the audience's viewpoint this only gives an impression of chaos. It's a little as though you were observing some important event using a pair of binoculars, which you constantly turned around so that part of the time you were seeing the event enlarged and close up, and the rest of the time far away. Thus the way one sees the event becomes more important than the event itself.

In order to avoid this danger, the director will have to choose the lenses used in consecutive takes in such a way that there is an impression of continuity, making it virtually impossible for the audience to tell when we pass from one take to the next, from one scene to another.

Cinema consists of drawing the audience's attention to the significant elements and eliminating the superfluous. What are the means we use to do this? I will mention three:

- Framing, which eliminates from the start what we don't want to show the audience
- Lighting, which leaves in darkness or shadow whatever might distract the audience's attention from the subject
- The movement of the camera, which, by heading toward the essential, will sweep aside the superfluous as it goes

All of this corresponds to our own way of perceiving the world, for we eliminate from our field of vision everything that does not hold or attract our attention: when we're looking for a phone number in our address book, our eyes move quickly past all the others till they light on the one we want. Brightly lighted subjects always draw our attention. When we are shifting our gaze from one object to another, we tend to move from one point to the other without letting anything in between interfere.

Here are a few points of reference that will give you a fair idea of how light and shadow can be used.

Take for example a face that is backlighted. The source of light, in other words, is behind the actor's head. The result is a face steeped in shadow and without expression, surrounded by a halo of light, with two possible variations: the background itself can be a shadowy or darkened wall, or a luminous sky. In either case, the effect, while different, will show the actors alone, or the actors and backdrops, in silhouette and shadow, giving them an air of mystery.

It is in the nature of shadows to be ineffable, to erase every banal detail. We may know who the character is, but seeing him or her in shadow may suggest or reveal something different about that person. An unusual light lends new meaning to what seemed familiar.

Try this little experiment: look at a landscape into the sun, then turn and look in the opposite direction. In the first phase you'll get a general impression of the countryside in front of you; in the second, you'll be surprised how many more details emerge, distracting your attention from the overall view. The scene viewed with the sun at your back is multicolored, that viewed with the sun facing you will tend to be more black and white.

First let's apply the experiment to film. Look at a landscape with the sun at your back. There is a welter of objects, a chaotic scene from which you'll have to make a selection, focusing on those you want to emphasize. Now look at the same landscape through a 250-mm lens. You'll be surprised: the background, dotted with secondary elements, loses its aggressiveness. The image softens, the medley of colors melts into flat tints of color that appear sharper than they had to the naked eye. The foreground, however, is transformed into a colored haze that seems to float. This effect was masterfully used by the French director Claude Lelouche in his early films. I am indebted to him for revealing the possibilities of this technique to me, which I used in my 1968 film *Everything for Sale.* In fact, my director of photography, Witold Sobocinski, called these colored, imprecise objects that appeared in the foreground "lelouches."

For each scene in a film you have to choose the right time of day or night. This choice depends on the story line, of course, but you can also use this element—day or night, dawn or dusk—to connote something to the audience.

As I indicated earlier, the sequence of light and dark, of day and night, is used by the scriptwriter and director to indicate the passage of time. Think of Fellini's *La Strada,* whose very title, "The Road," implies something fleeting, a transience expressed on-screen by the alternating scenes shot in daylight and at night.

Night scenes, either outside or in dark interiors, unfortunately often look as if the scenes had been shot in dull daylight, which is not only bad filmmaking but can throw the audience off. One simple way of taking care of this problem is to include a source of light in your frame. When seen on-screen, that light source will indicate the direction from which the light is coming: from a window, from a lamp, from the sky. It will also give the audience an idea of the time of day or night. An unlighted light bulb in the frame of a well-lighted window shows you it's daylight; the opposite, a lamp or electric light against a darkened window is, of course, nighttime. A mundane example, but the filmmaker has constantly to be aware of the simple, little, implicit signals he has to send the audience to avoid having to "tell" everything explicitly. A darkened window doesn't automatically mean night: if the preceding scene depicted a dark and stormy day, the following interior may have a darkened window and still be high noon. Only the context will tell the audience for sure. If there is any doubt, the director must make sure to orient the audience, using a lighted lamp or a flickering candle, to tell them that the scene is truly taking place at night.

In the heart of a forest, the lighting is always from the sky, whether it's day or night. Through filters you can create the effect of both day and night in forest situations: the only difference is that at night, shadows will erase the details, and the sky itself will appear dark rather than light. This method of using filters, making sure the sky doesn't show, to create the illusion of darkness is called "American night." Just make sure that in such situations your actor is carrying a burning torch to light his way!

Lots of on-screen "nighttimes" are actually shot during the day. Take the example of a cloudy day. Add some artificial rain and a waiting carriage, its lantern lights reflected in the glistening pavement. We see the street, the horses, the carriage—all of which are essential to the action of the story. But what tells us the time, and is the dominant detail of the scene, are the carriage lamps and their reflections. There you have it: a nighttime scene shot in broad daylight.

26

Don't Forget to Light the Eyes!

When I was a young student at the Academy of Fine Arts in Cracow, my old professor Karol Frycz used to tell us that one of the most serious crimes the theater had ever committed in the name of "modernity" was to eliminate footlights at stage level. The reasoning was that those lights created an improper and unnecessary barrier between the actors and the public. The only problem was, by eliminating those lights, the audience could no longer see the actors' eyes. And if you loved the actors, Professor Frycz used to lament, how could you deprive the audience of the very light that made their eyes sparkle onstage? Eyes that are capable of expressing everything: hope, sorrow, love! So much can be discerned through the eyes of a good actor. Are the eyes not, as the saying goes, the mirror of the soul? When it comes to film, the audience can only decipher what is depicted in that mirror if the eyes are lighted as they should be.

Lighting the eyes is a difficult art. It demands complex manipulations by the cameraman, manipulations that often have a prejudicial effect on some of his original lighting concepts, and which can even spoil some of the effects he was striving for. How do you compensate for a situation where the actor is being tracked or chased by the camera? The answer is that you have to concoct all sorts of ingenious methods to balance the needs of the action and the aesthetics of the eyes. If you love actors, you must never let this detail slide or be forgotten. They will be eternally grateful to you for doing so. Remember what Hamlet said about actors: "After your death you were better have a bad epitaph than their ill report while you live."

27

The Useless Chair Marked "Director"

In shooting any script, it's not only its action, plot, and content that we are shooting. Any scene in any script can appear on-screen filled with freshness and energy—or boredom and indifference, depending on the degree of commitment the entire film crew bring to it. The director can accomplish nothing alone. His concepts and emotions will be brought to fruition not only by the actors but by the crew. If the set is imbued with a feeling of slowness, boredom, and pretension, all these elements will somehow creep into the film itself and show up on-screen. That is why an experienced director will always choose his colleagues slowly and carefully, and try to weld them into a cohesive team. This crew must first of all be persuaded that they are involved with a winner. Only the director can instill that faith in the crew, providing the example himself, right on the set.

Between the ages of twenty-seven and fifty-five, I have been ill for a grand total of five days. There were only three times I was unable to show up on the set. For the actors and crew alike, the director has to symbolize solidity, a fixed point of reference. Everything else may fall apart: the weather, the actors' health, the working conditions, but the director must be on his feet on the set all the time, in wind or rain, ready to take care of whatever questions arise.

Did I say "on his feet"? I did indeed. Both in the theater and in filmmaking that is a self-imposed rule I have never broken (to the frequent astonishment of many in this rather sedentary world). Elia Kazan recalls the pioneer American film directors, their legs cased in leather and spread wide, standing as they directed. We've all seen photos of D. W. Griffith or Eric von Stroheim on the set, striding, gesticulating, always on their feet: for me that expresses the American films of energy and action that I love and admire above all others.

I have often seen the well-known director's chair. I have even seen a director stretched out on a couchlike contraption, studying the shooting script. What a sorry spectacle!

On the set, the director is the source of energy and inspiration to everyone, actors and crew. If he spends half his time sprawled in a comfortable chair, his energy level will inevitably drop, and that in turn will have a stultifying effect on everyone involved.

28

The Director
in Search of Confirmation

In the course of shooting I'm always on the lookout for ways of making sure the work is going well. By all means, I would like to know ahead of time the truth that will ultimately only be revealed by the public when the film is finally released. It is difficult to analyze the infinite number of elements that will determine whether or not a film will be a success. If a computer could be programmed to make that determination, studios would have been using them long ago (although for all I know, maybe they have). As for myself, a director of meager financial resources, I have had to set up my own personal system.

From the moment I started to make films when I was twenty-seven, I developed a duodenal ulcer (the classical illness of film-makers). I still have to treat it, but the positive side of this painful coin is that it serves me as an infallible barometer. If in the course of shooting or viewing the rushes, the pain becomes acute, then I know the scene is a success! It's obvious: if my ulcer acts up, it's because of the emotion or feeling the scene has aroused in me, and I can be quite sure it will have the same effect on the audience later on—although they won't have the pain.

During the shooting of *The Orchestra Conductor*, I had occasion to raise hell with my assistants, who for some reason, probably having to do with inexperience, had disappeared from the set. Sir John Gielgud was in complete approval of my outburst; it was the mark of a good director. He approved not because I was raising hell with them per se but because he saw that I had roused myself without losing control. That is the key for any director: to direct your dissatisfaction outward; it can be violent as long as it is sincere. You have to know how to shake other people up without ever losing your own self-control. If a director simply loses his temper, he will also run the risk of not being in control of his work and, instead of spurring the crew to increase their efforts, chances are he will harm the film.

In my view, the director should always see the rushes not only with cast and crew but with anyone else who wants to see them. It will show that you're aware that the film is not yours but theirs, that it's a joint effort; it will also demonstrate that you have nothing to hide. There will inevitably come a day when the film will be shown to the public. Sharing the rushes with cast and crew is a way of preparing for that fateful moment. Even though the print may be less than perfect, the sound not yet what it should be, even though the projection equipment is not wonderful, you'll still derive from the rushes a *sense* of whether the film is moving in the right direction. If as you look at the screen you manage to forget your problems and get caught up in the action and the lives of the characters, you've succeeded.

When the shooting is over, when the entire film is, as they say, in the can, I gather my first public together: cast, crew, friends, plus a few people dragged in off the street. I show them the rough cut. Without question that is the surest way of getting confirmation. The film can be improved in the editing process, but the characters created by the actors and the rhythm of their performances cannot be changed. There is nothing anyone can do to remedy that problem, if indeed it exists; the basic success of the film can be obtained only on the set.

God created the world in six days, and on the seventh He rested, knowing that He had done His work well. In the same way, if the director has found a good subject and fashioned a script worthy of it, if he has cast the film well and gathered around him a dedicated crew, he has nothing to fear: the film will be a success.

This said, it is not all that frequently that all these elements fall easily into place. Nevertheless, the director should also be careful not to feel so godlike that he has to interfere in every last detail. Even God, once He had finished His six-day creation, let the cattle graze in peace, the birds soar on their own wings, the fish swim in the waters of the earth. He knew that each species knew how to do what it had been created for. In the same way, the director cannot spend his time correcting everyone and everything forever. Even God allowed Adam and Eve to sin of their own free will, without His interfering.

I have been told that when Jean Renoir began shooting his *Grand Illusion* he was unhappy with Eric von Stroheim's performance. And yet we realize today that that performance is one of the high-water marks in the history of filmmaking. When I was making *Ashes and Diamonds*, if I had spent my time teaching or telling Cybulski how he should act in front of the camera, instead of watching him with wonder and admiration, I would have spoiled one of the great opportunities of my life. For in the final analysis, if you want to create something original, something that sets your film apart from all the others, you've got to let your colleagues—*especially* the actors—develop their own style in complete freedom.

29

And Where Does Art Fit into All This?

Where is there room for individual expression, for art, in all this? Nowhere! Even if you follow my advice and subject yourself to an absolute discipline, the results will not necessarily be artistic. Art is not something you can capture and pin down: a certain amount of disinterest, a certain independence toward your subject, are necessary if your film is to become a work of art.

Take the analogy of painting. In David's magnificent painting of Marat, the figure of Marat, dying in the bathtub, the knife having dropped to the floor, leads you to believe that the underlying principle of the composition is horizontal. I studied this painting very carefully when I was preparing to film *Danton*. The fact is, the composition is vertical! Above the dying man looms an enormous, empty space, which seems perfectly gratuitous. Why didn't David extend his painting out to the left? If he had done so, we doubtless would have caught a glimpse of Charlotte Corday running away from the scene of her crime. Or why didn't he extend it downward? If he had, we doubtless would have discovered the immense pool of blood that had poured from the veins of "the friend of the people." No, none of that! Guided by some sixth sense, David decided to paint, above the body of the murdered revolutionary, an immense, neutral, monochromatic background. Perhaps he had the feeling that after having painted the body of the assassinated revolutionary, the bathtub, the sheets of notes, and the knife of the murderess, his task as painter of the Revolution and friend of Marat was done. Perhaps too, as he was painting, he thought of the commonplace nature of death, and its inevitability (and revolutionaries die sooner than others): one could only speculate about what led him to paint that vast green space above the victim's head. Between the terms "disinterested" and "useless" there is an unfathomable depth. The vertical format of the painting *The Death of Marat* is arbitrary—and indispensable.

That is my reply to the question: where is the place for artistic license in a film? Everywhere. Wherever you find it.

30

Drunk or Sober?

One beautiful afternoon, after having finished shooting *Danton*, I climbed into the passenger seat of the cameraman's sports car. I asked him why he wasn't fastening his seat belt.

"Andrzej," Igor Luther responded, "I am no longer afraid of anything, even death. The only time I'm afraid is when we're shooting."

Yes! That's precisely it: the state of tension that has to exist between the cameraman and director. That tension electrifies the crew, infuses life into the cast; they all have the feeling that this is not just another film but that they are taking part in an important and unique event.

Fear doesn't have to be paralyzing. The wrong kind of fear can turn the director into a monster: he castigates cast and crew, as though by taking it out on them his own anxiety will be diminished. I heard of one director who demanded that the one tall, stately tree in the middle of a prairie be chopped down since that was the precise point where he had decided his camera had to be placed. There was another who insisted on dozens upon dozens of retakes, which is absurd and can only be attributed to his own sense of power. When you come right down to it, the director's only real strength is being constantly aware of what he has undertaken. That awareness allows him to be flexible in his demands and above all to admit, "I'm sorry, I don't know," or "I made a mistake."

The other professional defect (which is rife especially among less experienced directors) is to spend far too much time and effort on details. Everything, absolutely everything, seems important to them. They spend hours on some secondary effect that may not even be visible on-screen. They will spend hours on transitional scenes that in all likelihood will not survive the editing process, and they will wait for hours, while cast and crew sit idle, for some missing prop or object to be delivered, while the chances are they don't even need it. But this proves how meticulous they are, and how hard they work.

During my first year as a student at the Academy of Fine Arts, we used to spend our first hours in the composition course sketching the broad outlines of what we were drawing. The next day we would move on to the details, and by the third day we were down to the toenails and fingernails. Nothing could be more natural. Unless they start by concentrating all their talent and energies on the graphic and pictorial aspects of their painting, the students end up wasting even more of their time on unimportant details. The same holds true for filmmakers.

To avoid falling into that trap, I think the young filmmaker should work quickly. The errors that will crop up cannot be erased by perfecting details. By working quickly you can capitalize on something good, speed up the pace, inject a measure of intensity into the effort. If he allows himself too much time, the young filmmaker will get lost in words, become overly aware and conscious that he is *directing*—in other words, avoid the basics, sidestep the questions for which he doesn't yet have the answers.

Cézanne's watercolors, his interrupted drawings that were barely sketched out, are nonetheless perfectly finished works of art. All the problems of the relations between color and design, of nature reconstituted and translated to one-dimensional paper, have all been worked out and need no commentary as to how they might have been better if only the painter had had more time.

Isn't the same thing true of Sergei Eisensteins's *Que Viva Mexico!*? Each image on-screen reveals the piercing look, the boundless intelligence, of the Russian master. What a pity that he never had time to complete it! And yet, the unedited version is so strong and so compelling that it exists as a complete film in the minds of those who see it.

If the director is a sensitive man—and if he is not, how in the world can he ever hope to communicate his thoughts and feelings to others?—he must try to find ways to use the production process to express things that he has hitherto repressed. In countries such as Poland, I'm sorry to report, the method most often used to let go is vodka. But I have also seen directors in other countries "create" while under the influence. At first glance, one can readily understand how this happens and find it attractive. The director's euphoria is contagious. There's a lot of laughing on the set. The only thing is, scenes shot under these conditions seldom convey their good humor to the screen, for one very simple reason. I've seen directors drunk, but cameramen only rarely. I've even seen a whole crew under the influence—but I have never seen a drunk camera. And that is the key point, for the objectivity of the camera lens is legendary. If you want to force the camera to give a subjective look, you have to concentrate your most objective intelligence on it, impose your will implacably. Only a sober director can do that. And, you should remember, the audience viewing your film will be sober. A drunken film can only be shown to an audience of friends, and they should be well primed beforehand. But films such as those have nothing to do with the film profession. Leave them to amateurs filming a family barbecue.

31

I Was Kantor's
Assistant Director

As to those who, through curiosity or a desire to learn, would perhaps
of their own accord offer to help him, besides that their promises
generally exceed their performance, and that they stretch out fine
designs of which not one succeeds, they will undoubtedly expect to be
compensated for their trouble by the explication of certain difficulties
or, at least, by compliments and useless speeches, in which he cannot
spend any portion of his time without loss to himself.

> —Descartes,
> Discourse on Method, *Part VI*

The above quotation applies perfectly to assistant directors. I speak
out of personal experience, for I was one myself. I fully expected
that my contribution would be appreciated and that through that
job I would be initiated into the mysteries of the film world. I
quickly lost interest in the picture we were making as soon as I
realized that its outcome did not depend on me and that I was
not the moving force behind it.

And then after twenty-two years of working independently, I
had the experience of becoming an assistant director again for
one day. I was shooting *Man of Marble* in Cracow when I went
to see the stage production of Tadeusz Kantor's *The Dead Class.*
I had the immediate and overwhelming desire to preserve this
hair-raising spectacle on film. Kantor agreed to the experiment.
I wanted to shoot two or three exterior scenes—I thought that it
would broaden things a bit. But I also wanted to see how Kantor

101

would handle things as a film director. I was not disappointed. The three scenes were to be shot in the course of a single day: morning in full sunlight, dusk, and night. For the scenes of evening and night I had chosen as location the old tumbledown marketplace in the former Jewish quarter of Kazimierz.

First thing in the morning I asked my director what he needed for both these scenes. Not much, Kantor replied. It might be a good idea to scatter some paper about, make a huge garbage pile out of the set. He added that he happened to see as he was leaving his house that morning a truck full of corrugated paper—doubtless on its way to be recycled—and that if we could find the truck the cardboard might just do the trick. That was the only piece of information I could get out of him before the shooting began.

I immediately gathered my crew and, alternately threatening and begging (you never know which one will work the best), I ordered them to scour the city and find that truck. It took us a full day to shoot the first scene, and I had not had a moment even to think about the truck, much less ask if it had been found. But when Kantor and I arrived at the marketplace at dusk, there it was, with its heavy load of cardboard. I looked at Kantor and said, "Is that the truck?" Without a trace of surprise he said, "Yes," and without further ado it was unloaded.

The only problem was, once it was on the ground the cardboard simply looked like piles of . . . cardboard. No garbage effect at all. Kantor growled: "We'll have to wet it." As if by magic, a municipal watering truck was standing by, and with a wave of my hand I ordered it into action. Within moments the piles of cardboard were soaking wet. Even though we had scattered the cardboard as best we could throughout the set before soaking it, the new effect was hardly better than the old. Kantor seemed hesitant. I awaited his instructions.

"We'll have to set it on fire," he said.

Again I waved to my assistants. They ran throughout the

marketplace dousing the wet cardboard with gasoline. Was it too wet to ignite? No, only the top had been soaked, so soon the marketplace was glowing with the fire that had been set. But I could see that Kantor had already lost interest. He had understood that no matter what we did this cardboard was just not going to work.

As for myself, I was thinking what a thankless role the assistant director's is. He may be a genius, a demiurge who satisfies every whim of this monster, the director, fulfills his every demand in the twinkling of an eye, and do you think the ogre is grateful or thanks him? Of course he doesn't. That's all part of the job.

32

The Editing Dilemma:
Cut or Keep?

Editing can be a creative process on one condition: you have to
have enough material to begin with so that the director and film
editor have real options, real choices among various possible
solutions, so that the choices become highly personal.

A director once told me that he had edited his film in the
course of a single afternoon, a total of five to seven hours in all,
for the entire picture consisted of fifteen takes of several hundred
feet each. The theory of editing as you shoot eliminates the notion
of creating one scene using several takes. In my view, that method
is inconsistent with the diversity of rhythm that is part and parcel
of the art of filmmaking, and that diversity can only be obtained
by breaking the action up into multiple takes.

A film that is made using long, uninterrupted takes can pride
itself on an impressive unity of style, but most of the time it is
unrelievably boring. Not too long ago that style was all the rage,
and highly considered. I tried it myself, and I came to the conclusion that that method of filmmaking poses no special problems, even for a relatively inexperienced director, for it requires
less imagination, less technical knowledge (and above all less
time) than it does to shoot a scene using a number of takes. There

is also no question that the latter method is more demanding, since the task is to maintain the unity of style, acting, action, and lighting while you interrupt the shooting.

If on the set a particular scene is formless, if you have run out of ideas about how you give it the special effect you know it deserves, there is no point trying to hide it from the crew. There are days when inspiration refuses to strike, but that does not mean you have to be any less in charge; you're still the director. In situations like this I always try to photograph the action and the actors as precisely as possible, in multiple takes: long shots at first, medium next, then close-ups. I am well aware that this method might appear to be the very antithesis of art. But it does give me the opportunity, later on in the editing room, to come back to that scene and think it through at that later stage.

Many directors stifle their editors' work by resisting cuts, which they feel is cutting their own memory. They think: if you make that cut, how can I ever re-create what I was trying to capture on the set? You have to rid yourself of that fear.

There is another danger as well: that the director clings to the idea that he has of his film, whereas the material that has already been edited tells him something different, that something new has emerged from the editing process that should be recognized and taken into account. It is as though the commander of an army persisted in his initial battle plan despite the disconcerting news he received from the front.

The daily rushes give us a certain idea of our work and how it is progressing. But only the edited version of several scenes will show us the real face of the film to come. It will provide the possibility of making certain indispensable corrections while the film is still being shot. It gives us a chance to see which actor is really making a forceful impression, and what we need to do to compensate for those whose performances are not up to scratch. In short, if you edit the film as you go along, while you are still shooting, you should be able to have a fully edited version a week after the shooting is finished, while there is still time to go back and reshoot certain scenes or add some scenes that, in the light of what you have seen, are necessary. You can do so because your crew is still available.

Here's a piece of advice for the hesitant. A young filmmaker thinks that it would be all but impossible for him to go back and shoot a scene that the dialogue would seem to call for, or a close-up that is missing, anywhere but on the original location. Wrong. You can add new takes to an already finished scene virtually anywhere, on condition that before you do, you examine the scene frame by frame so that you make sure you know each background exactly. During my many years in film, I have shot hundreds and hundreds of such retakes either in the offices of the producer or in the courtyard of a studio, and that includes not only interiors but also retakes and additional takes of scenes that took place in a birch forest or at the edge of a lake. I know that the level of the actors' performance is far more important than the perfection of the background.

Among the most difficult conflicts a director will have to fight in the editing room is facing up to the necessity of cutting material. You almost always have to. The excess of material is the natural result of the shooting process. Some scenes are expanded; others are added because in the course of events they seem necessary, even though they weren't in the original script. The ideal solution would be to eliminate the weakest scenes; unfortunately these are often essential to the action and understanding of the picture. Thus you have to keep those scenes, knowing full well they are not as strong as they should be, while at the same time eliminating others of which you are proud because they are strong and interesting but, nevertheless, useless in the context of the film.

Never try to favor those scenes in your film that you thought were the most powerful at the time you were first working with the script. On the contrary. Try to attain the level of ideal film-making in the scenes that, at first sight, strike you as the least interesting. That will prevent you from grappling with the agonizing dilemma of what you have to eliminate in the editing room: the subject matter, or art.

33

The Truth of Sound
Participates in the Truth
of the Picture

In 1954, when I was making my first film, sound tracks were still being recorded on the film itself. Looking back, the strangest thing was that we had the means to utilize this material in the final mixing, while at the same time we tried not to add other sounds to the dialogue itself to make sure it could be heard.

Since the invention of magnetic tape for sound recording—and that was a major revolution in cinematic production—we no longer have that concern. The sound recorded at the time of shooting serves only as a reference for our later needs. Once the shooting is over, the actors rerecord their dialogues in the controlled confines of a studio, not only synchronizing their words but reliving and re-creating the passions and feelings they expressed at the time of the shooting.

That method evolved as the result of two firm beliefs:

1. The crew tends to be noisy on the set during takes. On the set, the director should be free to communicate freely with the actors, the cameraman, and his assistants. In the end, the only thing that matters is the quality of the image.

2. The final recording of the dialogues should be done under studio conditions, where calm reigns and where the director can work on making sure all the inflections and nuances are both properly spoken and properly recorded, in other words re-creating in final form what was only sketched out on the set itself.

These were merely presumptions, but in fact over the past several years we've never been able to get rid of them despite the technical advances that have been made in sound recording equipment that would enable us to record our sounds impeccably on the set.

What finally convinced filmmakers that they need not resort to postsynchronization was the impact of television, with its live interviewing and reporting. Filmmakers were suddenly struck by the naturalness of the dialogues, the spontaneous vocabulary, forceful despite its repetitions and sputtering. The first people to make use of this "new" method were the documentary directors, followed closely by the pioneer directors of the *cinéma vérité* school, and after them the whole industry. People in the profession realized that there was a profound and mysterious concordance between sound and picture—however difficult it was to say just what it was—when they were recorded simultaneously.

When I was shooting *Promised Lands*, the weaving machines of the textile mill were making thousands of yards of cloth, and the noise was deafening. The actors were obliged to deliver their lines much more forcefully than usual. The problem was, when we later tried to re-create that same feeling in the sound studios we couldn't do it: only the noise of the machines had enabled the actors to achieve those effects naturally.

Today there are many sophisticated means of going about the postsynchronization process (and more are being invented all the time), but in my view the initial sound recording is irreplaceable and therefore you have to come back to what the sound operator has done on the set in the presence of the director.

I know from experience that independently of the technical quality and precision of the dialogues, sound has to appear on-screen in absolute synch with the image. At the stage of rushes, this process should already be well in place. No matter what your plans for postsynchronization may be, the various sound takes—near, far, background, offscreen—should be done precisely and accurately during the shooting. It would be wrong to think that the possibilities of the sound studio are limitless. Speaking for myself, I have been disappointed in the results I have obtained in the postsynchronization process.

The countless sounds recorded "naturally" that have no direct relation to the picture are difficult to identify. Our sound environment is replete with a number of apparently insignificant elements. But that is precisely why well-recorded dialogues done on the set, the sounds and background noises that are there naturally, can provide—in association with the image—the perfect illusion of space and depth that you cannot match in any sound-recording studio no matter how hard you try or how sophisticated the equipment at your disposal.

I have also noted that if the sound operator has too broad a range of possibilities at his disposal, there is a good chance the mixing will be "unclean." Again, I think of the painter who cannot make up his mind which color to use and as a result mixes too many colors on his palette, and as a consequence ends up with a muddy painting.

34

Music,
Not Musical Illustration

I have no formal musical training, and of all my limitations that is the one I regret the most. And yet I do not always work with the same composer, as do a number of my colleagues who, aware of their own lack of musical knowledge, are afraid to experiment. I try my luck with different composers, depending on the subject and character of my film. I have, therefore, of necessity been led to form an opinion on the role of music in filmmaking and how it works, if only to make sure I don't go about this aspect of the art blindly.

The function of music in movies has undergone a profound evolution in the course of the past few years. When I was starting out in my career, the composer would begin by viewing the film several times in the editing room. After that we would pinpoint those places where music would occur: which takes for which music would be specially composed, and timed to the second. We called that process "musical illustration," and in the same way that Gustave Doré's illustrations precisely matched the text of the books he illustrated, like *Don Quixote* or *The Divine Comedy*, so our composers correlated their notes to our images.

Today things are completely different. The composer is involved with the film from the start of shooting. Thus his inspiration does not derive from the fully edited film; rather he participates in the creative process right along with the director. I think that is far and away the best way of working, for the composer's own creative process coincides with that of the picture itself, rather than having to adapt to the finished product.

There has also been a major evolution in our collective sensitivity to music over the past few years. I ascribe that change to the widespread use throughout the world of the transistor radio. We listen to Vivaldi as we drive our car. At the same time our ears are sensitive to the purr of the motor and the conversation of the passengers in the car. Today that is generally the way we listen to music. It goes with us everywhere, a constant companion to whatever we're doing. It doesn't illustrate anything. It is there, independent, an integral part of our lives. That accompaniment often bears little or no relation to how we feel or where we are.

Years ago, as he was boarding a plane to the accompaniment of Muzak, the pianist Arthur Rubinstein said to me: "Oh no! There's that music again! What if I were on my way to a funeral?"

Thus it is that music mixed with other sounds, music neither desired nor necessarily appropriate, is part and parcel of our environment. Because of all this it is not surprising that today's film composers use scraps, fragments, "spots" instead of the musical illustration of earlier times, that precise, homogeneous music that corresponded to the action of the picture.

Another "discovery" has been to superimpose over the picture fragments of classical music. The initial results were charming and impressive. The screen could be filled with ordinary images and insignificant actors. No matter! The harmonies of Bach or Brahms or Vivaldi lent them depth, mystery, and next to such music, the dialogues faded or blurred, the other superfluous noises disappeared altogether. The magic of the old masters reigned supreme. Unfortunately, this bliss lasted for a very short time.

112

All these pictures began to blur into one, as the music swallowed up the personality of the director, the scriptwriter, and the actors, transforming the cinema into a series of pictures illustrating the eternal music.

Given all the above, the composer who works in the medium of film knows that henceforth:

1. His music, even if it relates to certain scenes and sequences, may be moved elsewhere in the editing process. Thus he must try to find a musical theme that fits the film in a general way and also sets it apart from all the others. Therein will lie his creative efforts, rather than in trying to match his music to a specific scene as he did in the past.

2. His music will meld into the dialogue and the sounds that emanate naturally from the action portrayed, and therefore there is no point in approaching the work as though it were a finished product as in the past. (One thinks, for example, of Eisenstein's adjusting—or so the story goes—the images of *Alexander Nevsky* and *Ivan the Terrible* to fit Prokovie's music.)

My own experience has given me insights into another aspect of film music altogether. No matter how intrinsically interesting or compelling a film because of its plot or story, any audience tends to get tired by virtue of the length of the picture itself. If a good director can pinpoint those moments when the audience has probably had enough and add music at those key points, he can resuscitate the spectators' interest in the dialogue, the human word. Since films today are becoming longer and increasingly wordy, that use of music becomes all the more important.

All of which brings me to ask the question: why is it that films today are becoming longer? There are many reasons, but among them is the fact that people like to remain seated for long stretches in movie houses or in front of their television sets, rather than taking part in real life. Many years ago when I made my film *Ashes and Diamonds*, a very long two-part work, I was afraid of the public's reaction. I expressed my fear to a Polish writer who said to me, "What I'd like to see you make is a film so long I'd never have to leave the theater." There were several reasons for his fear of life and his wish to hide in a dark movie theater. Not long thereafter he committed suicide.

If most films require music, I think it is safe to say that in long films that element is absolutely essential. In any event, we directors automatically assume that if we are making a film, music is part of the equation.

Is music indispensable? As far as my own films are concerned—those in which I knew where I was going and what I wanted to achieve—I knew in advance what music would best support the story. For *Ashes and Diamonds*, what I wanted were the ordinary songs of the day that could be heard in the hotel rooms and restaurants in which the key scenes of the picture took place. For *Promised Lands*, on the contrary, I knew that it needed a major composer fully capable of writing for a symphony orchestra, because of the huge number of characters, the number and diversity of the settings, and the complexity of the plot. I found that composer in the person of Wojciech Kilar. His music reinforced the crowd scenes and those that took place in the factories, as well as added an ironic note to the scenes of worldliness. *Danton*, to take another example, makes use of an apparently anachronistic modern music composed by Jean Prodromides, which succeeds in capturing the essence of the picture: the sense of things tearing apart.

Some people say that good film music is inaudible. That may be another way of complimenting the composer by saying that he has done his job so well one is not aware of the music as an outside element.

35

Why I Work in the Theater

My first requirement when working in the theater is to choose a text that has withstood the test of time, that has become immortal. I try as best I can to understand what Shakespeare, Chekhov, or Strindberg is telling me. I never touch these texts; I don't try to "improve" the scenes; I do not change a word of dialogue; I never adapt. For weeks on end I read and reread the text with the actors, firmly believing I will find an answer. This process makes me a better director, more attentive and more ambitious, for I know that many other directors before me have gone through the same process, with the same hope of unraveling the mystery. These analytical rehearsals, carried out in peaceful surroundings, give us a better chance of understanding the mysteries of *Hamlet*, the confusion of *The Three Sisters*, the implacable logic and fantastic construction underlying the events of Ibsen's *Peer Gynt*.

In theatrical productions, the director must faithfully follow the text. His discoveries will only be in the context of a deeper understanding of what the author intended: thus his role is limited, while that of the film director is vast.

In the theater there is no escape: the actors are right there, so close I can touch them. I must endure their gazes, respond to their questions (even if the answer is "I don't know"). I can't hide behind my camera, which I often do when I am shooting a picture, or refer them to my assistants.

In the theater the actor is aware from the moment he first sets foot onstage that he is responsible for the performance. That knowledge makes him sure of his own worth, whereas many actors who play in films have the feeling that they are simply cogs in the enormous wheels of the machine known as the cinema.

Critical rehearsals, exercises, rehearsals onstage, conversations in the theater and elsewhere, all bring me closer to the actors and help me to get to know them better, to know more about them than is ever possible in the course of shooting a picture, where my relations with the cast are comparatively fleeting. Working in the theater, seated across the narrow table from the actors, I look them straight in the eye—for I know that there's no reason to conceal my lack of knowledge. Actors who spend most of their time working for films are another breed altogether, very fast on their feet, generally willing to offer their own solutions to any problems the director may have. They are both flexible and self-assured. The actors available for a film are not always the best, for movie actors tend to form a separate group and seem to reappear in all the films we see. In my opinion, introducing new faces is mandatory from time to time. But keeping abreast of the actors' "market" is not the main reason for working in the theater. Far more important, the theater teaches me many things, first and foremost being honest with the cast. And as I suggested, the theater provides no technical refuges from reality the way the cinema does very often. "Don't worry, it will look better once we've done the editing." "Wait till you see how that scene looks once we've added the music." "No, no, you'll never see that on screen."

Something else the theater does for me is to remind me constantly of the contradiction that I note between the "naturalness"

116

of the cinema, which imitates reality, and the "artifice" of the theater. Theater demands from the director a much sharper sense of form, the ability to pull together what is happening onstage into a coherent whole.

Some years back I was directing a stage production of Dostoyevsky's *The Possessed*. During the dress rehearsal, which took place on the day of the opening, one of the actors, as he was delivering his lines, grabbed the back of a chair in a way that struck me as *unreal* and, in a movement that struck me as equally *artificial*, collapsed onto the stage. Watching all that from my seat in the theater, I realized that something serious was going on and raced up onstage to help him.

The man was having a heart attack. Why did I initially think the man's movements "artificial"? Very simply because they were natural, and therefore not theatrical. That was not the way actors perform onstage, where reality has to be heightened and transposed. If this same event had occurred during the shooting of a film, I'm convinced I would have concluded that the actor had just figured out a fine new way of collapsing, that he was improvising, and I would doubtless not have rushed to his side.

Through such experiences as these, the theater has taught me to tell the difference between what is natural and what is true. Theater is the art of form. The imitation of life, which is essential for the cinema, does not suit its purposes. Theater takes place both on the stage and in the auditorium; the two indispensable elements are the actors and the audience. That is why the role of the director in the theater is relatively modest.

In one sense, the stage director should be viewed as someone who encourages and supports the actors, the person who is their first audience in the house during rehearsals. It is his job to make sure they work together harmoniously, and that their performances mesh. His role is also to know the play in depth, to understand its meaning and plot so thoroughly that he can place the proper emphases and establish the proper rhythm from start to finish. That may be viewed as a major contribution—or minor—depending on how one views the importance of that task as compared to the role of the author.

I am often asked why I devote so much of my time to the stage, that ephemeral art that vanishes as soon as the performance is over, since I could, if I wanted, spend that much more time making films, which are destined to endure, to move and amuse generations to come? And my answer is that it is the fleeting and provisional aspect of the theater that makes me love it so deeply. If we aspire to immortality, if in our heart of hearts we would like to be remembered long after we are gone, then death and oblivion also hold a certain fascination, a fascination that only increases as we age.

36

Two Kinds of Censorship

As is well known, there are two kinds of censorship. One is an internal censorship, which the artist imposes on himself, generally out of fear of the unknown. The other is an external censorship imposed by the various institutions in a country that see it as part of their role to keep order and uphold moral standards.

Too often censorship is thought of in terms of the restrictions imposed on artists and creators by the state, especially if the state finances their projects, which makes them in a sense state employees. That is an oversimplification. True censorship derives from the fear of exceeding the boundaries of decency, the tastes of the time, the social and moral prejudices.

When I was young I remember watching for the first time Louis Malle's *The Lovers*, mesmerized, gasping for breath. The film embodied for me a boundless erotic freedom. Much later, Oshima's *In the Realm of the Senses* taught me that in this realm there are no boundaries.

I have often talked to foreign journalists who wanted me to explain to them just how political censorship worked in Poland. But I could never get a satisfactory answer from any of them about why there were so few films made in France on politically charged or sensitive subjects such as the Algerian War or the events of May 1968. Does internal censorship take the place of political censorship?

Here is a fragment from a confidential document relating to Polish censorship:

II. Reference Number
ZI-Pf-132/18/75

Warsaw, July 16, 19—
Confidential
Copy #24

Censorship Inquiry No. 18

I enclose herewith, for the attention of the censorship committee, the text "remarks relative to the discussion concerning A. Wajda's *Promised Lands*," which the Department of Ideological and Educational Action of the Central Committee of the United Polish Workers' Party has written.

Julian Pelczarski
Director

A. Wajda is one of four Polish film directors who have achieved worldwide recognition. He is one of two (the other is Zanussi) who continues to work in Poland. His cinematic and theatrical creations, as well as the interviews he has granted, show that he is not politically involved in a pro-Marxist sense. Rather he has adopted a viewpoint that is not all that uncommon among artists—that of an "objective judge" of both the past and the present—it being his opinion that he has the right and the possibilities to apply the standards of humanism and morality to the problems of the world without having to resort to Marxism or any other philosophical or social system.

120

Film is an art that is aimed at the masses. All those intent on or involved in directing those masses cannot fail to be interested in this art. Necessarily, therefore, the film director finds himself situated between the public, whose feelings he wants to express, and the powers-that-be. No doubt somewhere in the world there are countries where such is not the case. But most often, in such places, boredom is so deeply entrenched that the most blood-curdling scream, coming from the very depths of the soul, scarcely makes an impression. No one expects it.

In Shakespeare's *Richard III*, the king is depicted, to say the very least, unfavorably. Now, historians have shown us that in the light of the historical evidence it is possible to view Richard III very differently. In England there exists, and has existed for a very long time, an association dedicated to restoring Richard III's good name. Needless to say, that association has not accomplished much. It is difficult to change the image of someone whose name and reputation have been fixed for all time in a work of drama, even though the play may be politically unfair, especially if the dramatist is Shakespeare. The association's facts may be correct, but what they lack is the myth.

This is exactly what the authorities fear: that the artist will portray the world according to his own vision without taking into account historical necessity, the dilemmas of power, the "extremely complex" political circumstances. In order to avoid this "problem," the Socialist state finances every kind of artistic production—from literature to film.

As I made my films throughout the years, I always had to submit them to the censors. I cut scenes, and above all dialogues, because for the censors the word is the privileged channel of ideology. Fortunately for people in my profession, film is image, or more precisely that impalpable "something" between image and sound which is the soul of film. Of course cuts can be made in *Ashes and Diamonds*, the words or exchanges of this character or that, but there is no way anyone can censor Zbyszek Cybulski's performance. It is precisely the way he is that contains that certain "something" representing political obscenity, the freedom of the boy in dark glasses confronting the reality imposed upon him. The same is true for *Man of Marble*. This film was inadmissible everywhere in the world. What could a few cuts do to it?

The main problem with political cinema is not whether you accept the meddling of the censors or not. The real problem is how to conceive of a work that will render them inoperative. No one can censor what he cannot understand, what transcends the imagination. Create something truly original and the censors will be completely lost; they will have to hang up their scissors and go home.

37

For How Much?
The Artist Vis-à-vis Power

The artist who wants to free himself—if only partially—from that schizophrenic situation must reply to this question: Who is he dependent on? For what money is he making his film?

If the film industry belongs to the state, it seems only fair that the ministry in charge oversees how the money it hands out is being used. We can nonetheless presume that in a Socialist country movies belong to the people, that is, the people ascribe to creative artists a portion of their income so that they—in this instance filmmakers—can make movies corresponding to their wants and needs.

There is a basic difference between these two conceptions, for in the case of a popular film industry the interference of the authorities would be superfluous—the filmmakers would direct their own affairs.

Among the many peculiar events of May 1968 in France was an all-night meeting of people working in the film industry. The subject being discussed was, essentially, the possibility of a new form of cinema in France: if television was financed by the fees paid by the people who owned TV sets, then why wouldn't it be possible to have some sort of collective financing of the movie industry? Imagine, for example, that every citizen would pay twenty-five dollars a year and for that have the right to see every film made in France for free. That proposal was turned down by the filmmakers themselves. One of them pointed out that such an arrangement would not really be "free cinema" in the sense intended but rather "obligatory cinema."

That story applies to our situation as well. Even if our production is financed by the state, we do not want an "obligatory cinema" in Poland! The question we have to answer is: who is the rightful producer of our films? The state is hardly the right body, since it is the producer who is directly responsible for making the film. The Ministry of Culture is only the means by which the authorities maintain control. But who is responsible to the citizens themselves? The answer is obvious: individually, all the directors, and collectively, the filmmakers' board of directors.

For the Polish Cultural Congress that took place from December 11 to 13, 1981, I had prepared the following text, entitled "State Protection and the Freedom of the Artist":

My Friends:

Today I would like to talk to you about how I view the role of the state as a protector of and patron of the arts, from my viewpoint as a Polish film director. I apologize for speaking especially about film, but the state plays different protective roles and has different kinds of involvement in the various realms of artistic endeavor. There are areas where its role is minimal, others where you can virtually ignore it.

You can, for instance, think at no cost whatsoever. And the cost of writing a novel is ridiculously low. Think of Stachura writing his absolutely stunning novel *Reconciling Yourself with Life*, one of the great works of Polish literature. The "cost" was a few pencils and half a dozen note-books. Or take the case of the painter Andrzej Wroblewski, who during the 1950s painted a series of watercolors entitled *Crucified to Chairs*—works that were as important as they were powerful, as beautiful as they were enduring. The cost was in terms of material more than Stachura's novel but still small by any standards.

When it comes to the world of film, unfortunately, we are dealing with millions, no matter what the subject may be.

Today, on the occasion of our Cultural Congress, I would like to reflect for a moment on what strikes me as a curious fact. To finance my films, the state has taken several million zlotys from the National Treasury. Now, as far as my artistic conscience is concerned, I do not feel I have contracted any obligation toward this state Maecenas. Does that mean that by taking the money and giving nothing back I have betrayed the state? Have I lied to it? No! Because while I did take public funds, I also used them in the service of the public. I knew that the Polish people needed my films. How did I know it? Very simple: by the number of tickets sold, the full houses my movies drew. That is the surest sign of a cinema considered to be "necessary."

One could argue that a great many bad films are commercially successful, far more successful than *Kanal, Ashes and Diamonds*, or *Man of Marble*. This is surely true, but it is also as certain that there is no way films could ever serve any useful public purpose if the theaters were empty, or if the only audiences who went and applauded were the servants of the state.

So I took the money offered me by the state in all good conscience, for I never considered it was my money in the first place. I always made sure that the money found its way back to the source whence it came, namely the National Treasury.

In Western countries, the person who manages to raise the money for the film is the producer, and that person is generally thought of as the creative force behind the picture. That person dictates how the film should be made. But when I was still quite young I learned the highest value is work. In our country the creators of films can only be people who work the hardest on it: the crew and the director. The notion of self-management that has existed in Poland for many years is in fact responsible for the flowering of the Polish film industry since the end of World War II.

I have never been overly concerned about the reactions of the authorities, pro or con, when it came to my films. My real concern was the public, especially if I was not succeeding in communicating with it.

It is high time to talk about what that freedom has meant to me. Why must any artist be free? The only reason I wanted to be free was to be able to penetrate the minds and hearts of my fellow citizens, to be able to express their hopes and worries, their illusions! The state Maecenas could not have done it all alone. Why would some functionary have a clearer idea of what this secret was than I? Because he was a functionary? I doubt very seriously that the peaceful offices of bureaucrats or scripts that are written collectively, debated, and voted on by common consent, will ever give birth to revealing works of art. On the contrary, communal discussions of this nature generally give rise to the worst lemons, faceless and soulless abortions.

The artist alone is responsible for what he says to the public. That is the way he expresses his freedom. There are times when an artist feels obliged to tell the public things it does not want to hear. He needs a sort of double freedom, freedom from the authorities and freedom from the public. Only major artists succeed in attaining that freedom, and to them we must be eternally grateful. As for Maecenas, whoever he may be, let him constantly bear in mind that if the cinema has flowered in Poland, it is only because the people have managed to wrest from the authorities a number of major concessions.

That was the speech I had prepared and was scheduled to deliver on December 13, 1981. But when we arrived at the lecture hall we found it closed and locked. A number of participants at the congress were arrested. Maecenas had decided to declare war on us!

Since the "thaw" of 1955–56, film professionals have done their best to promote the idea of an original structure based on "Groups of Cinematic Creation." Our public calls for different kinds of pictures. Is one overall "Film Office" capable of satisfying all those various needs? Of course not! That diversity can only be satisfied by a structure that allows filmmakers—all of whom are very different from one another—to express themselves freely in accordance with their temperaments and talents, their visions and viewpoints. The "Groups of Cinematic Creation" represent that structure in Poland.

Each such group is headed by three seasoned filmmakers: an artistic director (always a director); a literary director, who is a writer, scriptwriter, or critic; and a production director. I have an ideal production chief in the person of Barbara Pec-Slesicka, who has a profound understanding of the creative requirements and the mechanics of filmmaking.*

*Cinema Group X, directed by Andrzej Wajda, was dissolved by the authorities in 1982.—Trans.

These three people form the core of the group, to which other film people come of their own free will: other directors, set designers, and production people. Part of each group's role is to recruit recent graduates of our film school.

The artistic directors of a group are responsible for the group's productions: they commission scripts, discuss them with the authors, negotiate with the various official parties concerned with filmmaking, until they get the go-ahead to make the picture in question. Then the group is involved in overseeing the shooting, the editing, and, finally, in making sure the finished film gets the best possible distribution.

Long experience has shown us that this is the only way to guarantee the production of high-quality films, in which both the basic interests of the creators and the overall interests of the film profession are protected. This method can only work under one condition: that the groups are made up of artistic directors freely chosen, not imposed from above by the state. Without self-management the system will simply never work.

38

That Sad Day: The Premiere

The opening night of a film is a sad day for the director. If the picture is a success, he will look around at the group of friends who were responsible for making it so and realize that he will never work together again with all these same people and with the same spirit that infused our group during the preceding weeks and months. If on the contrary the film is a dud, he will begin picking it apart from that same opening night onward, finding errors everywhere. In either case, an opening night party is in order, with everyone invited, actors, production crew, technicians, and friends. Foreseeing the possibility of a disaster, one always makes sure to order in a sufficient amount of vodka.

Opening night is the final adieu to the picture. The director ought to be already thinking about his next film, which helps alleviate the feeling of emptiness that always follows a period of enormous concentration and tension. Opening night is also a period for looking back, for reflection on what has brought you to this point in your life and career.

When I was a student at the National Film School at Lodz from 1949 to 1953, I thought my studies were a waste of time. Many years later I learned that it was considered to be the best film school in the world. This leads me to pause for a moment and comment on the whole notion of teaching filmmaking.

I am convinced that the weak point in any educational system used to teach film lies in the fact that cinema is an art of compilation. Sometime back, opera was considered the consummate theatrical art, for it included all the other arts. That belief, or perhaps more properly, infatuation, did not serve opera in good stead, for the simple reason that it did nothing to help ensure the future development of the opera. Are films destined to suffer a similar fate? I suspect they are.

The formation of any artist ought to be accomplished through a single discipline, if the future artist's goal is to learn the art, not simply the technique. My advice to young would-be filmmakers is to apprentice themselves in three arts: music, literature, and painting. Each one of these areas has a link to the world of film, and through these related studies the student can draw his or her own conclusions.

Film schools pride themselves on teaching their students all three disciplines, once over lightly. The only problem is, music appreciation is not music, the history and theory of literature are not literature, the awareness of the graphic arts is not painting.

What I owe most to the Lodz school are the friendships I formed there, and that many of the people I have worked with through the years are graduates of that school. Edward Klosinski comes to mind: I knew him when he was an intern, then he became my assistant director, and then for several of my most recent films, a most valued working companion and my director of photography.

I owe my artistic education to the Academy of Fine Arts, but I must confess that the "best film school in the world" did not provide me with a great deal of practical training. I find it hard not only to recommend which school a would-be director ought to think of attending, but also even to come up with a meaningful career path to follow. In fact, I often wonder whether as a career or profession it is still as attractive and meaningful as it once was.

In Joseph Roth's wonderful novel *The Emperor's Tomb*, an elderly aristocrat, shocked to learn that his son's fiancée works in straw, cries out: "What is this world coming to when precious objects are being made out of such wretched materials!"

The modest means of most feature films and television programs have not, as we had hoped, given rise to either artistic or political freedom. All that impoverishment has done is to diminish the profession of directing, which offers up to the world not works of art but substitutes, of less and less intrinsic interest.

When I was young I had high hopes that we could change—and better—the world. Cinema—which is the art of the twentieth century—was to be one of the most effective ways for doing this. We believed that people of different countries and different races and different continents would learn to know one another through the art of the film, that knowing one another better would make them friends and allies. The fact is, the world today seems gravely ill, and no matter how many new toys are furnished to the spoiled children who play, they are never enough—and none seem destined to provide a cure.

Films made in Eastern Europe seem of little or no interest to people in the West. The audiences in western countries find them as antediluvian as the battle for workers' rights in England in the time of Marx. Thus our efforts here in Eastern Europe have nothing to show audiences in the West who look upon the world they live in as permanent. Those of our Eastern European film colleagues who have chosen emigration can—if they are young and talented and after they have spent years in the West—come up with some works of startling beauty, such as Milos Forman's *Amadeus*, but they will not find audiences attuned to the same concerns that we in the Eastern bloc feel are vital. And that is a pity, for I am certain that those concerns are not ours

131

alone but apply to the world at large, or will in the very near future.

The Iron Curtain is meaningless. Today the world is divided in two and the division seems solidly entrenched. But the symbol of the Iron Curtain, a 1950s phenomenon, is outdated.

Today there is no longer any place in the world of film for the universality of a Charlie Chaplin. That on both sides of this divided world films are shown nightly proves how vain were our youthful hopes that these divisions would crumble and disappear. There is no longer a cinema that addresses itself to everyone. And I must say that elitist films, those intended for the "happy few," I find unacceptable. In my view they represent the ultimate defeat.

That is why throughout this book I keep claiming kinship with the "public," why I continually want to identify with others. Sartre's phrase "Hell is other people" is not right for me. The others and I together represent the only strength, the only hope. I am dead set against the idea that the art of filmmaking is a mystery and the public a necessary evil, an element the true artist must endure.

That is why I joined the Polish union, Solidarity. I remain faithful to my ideal, for in that ideal I see the only remedy to our sterile solitude, to the emptiness that threatens so many people who seem ready and willing to sacrifice the common good for the sake of their own immediate comfort, people for whom the word "peace" seems nothing more than "leave me in peace," or "don't bother me."

Filmography

Generation
Kanal
Ashes and Diamonds
Lotna
The Innocent Sorceror
Samson
Fury Is a Woman
I Go Toward the Sun
Promised Lands
Everything for Sale
Love at Twenty
Without Anesthesia
The Dead Class
The Young Ladies from Wilko
Birchwood
Man of Marble
Man of Iron
The Orchestra Conductor
Landscape After the Battle
The Wedding
Danton
A Love in Germany

Author's Notes

ANDRZEJEWSKI, Jerzy: Writer, moralist, perfectionist. His novel *Ashes and Diamonds* (1947) served as the basis for my own film of the same title.

BROMOWICZ, Ryszard: Actor and director of my favorite stage theater, The Chemineau Theater in Cracow.

CYBULSKI, Zbyszek: Actor, who played in several of my films, including *Generation, Ashes and Diamonds*, and *Milosc dwudziestolakow* (*Love at Twenty*). I owe him what I consider to be the most successfully realized character in my work, that of Maciek Chelmicki in *Ashes and Diamonds*. The idol of Polish youth, Cybulski's tragic death in 1967 served as the inspiration for my film *Everything for Sale*.

DUNIKOWSKI, Xawery (1875–1964): A sculptor of genius. When I was young I made a documentary about his life and work entitled *Ide do slonca* (*I Go Toward the Sun*).

FALK, Feliks: Director, scriptwriter, member of my Cinema Group X. Author of the remarkable film *Wodzirej* (*The Playmaker*).

FRYCZ, Karol: Painter, set designer, stage director. He was my professor of set design at the Academy of Fine Arts in Cracow.

HOLLAND, Agnieszka: Director, and scriptwriter, she was the author of my film *Without Anesthesia*, and worked with me on *A Love in Germany*. Her own films are extraordinary: *Provincial Actors, Fever, A Woman Alone*. A person of exceptional and impeccable character, as only a woman can be. She has been living in Paris since 1981.

IWASZKIEWICZ, Jaroslaw: The doyen of Polish writers and poets, he dominated our literary scene without interruption from the 1920s up until his

134

death in 1980. He had one major theme: love and death. I based two of my films on his stories: *Birchwood* and *The Young Ladies from Wilko*.

JANDA, Krystyna: Actress, she played in several of my films: *Man of Marble, Man of Iron, The Orchestra Conductor, Without Anesthesia*. She was still a student when I discovered her vitality, her forcefulness, her dynamic personality, her inexhaustible energy.

KANTOR, Tadeusz: Painter, stage director, one of the principal movers and shakers of the Polish avant-garde. Overwhelmed by his stage production, *The Dead Class*, I filmed it in 1976, and for no apparent reason Kantor has never forgiven me.

KILAR, Wojciech: One of Poland's finest postwar composers. He composed the especially dynamic music for *Promised Lands*.

KLOSINSKI, Edward: Cameraman (*Promised Lands, Man of Marble, Without Anesthesia, The Young Ladies from Wilko, Man of Iron*). A consummate professional, he is also blessed with an innate dramatic sense. He is married to Krystyna Janda, whom he met while shooting *Man of Marble*.

LIPMAN, Jerzy: Cameraman. We began our careers together (*Generation, Kanal, Lotna, Ashes and Diamonds*). Polish cinema owes to him a whole new style of photography. He emigrated and worked in Germany and England until the time of his death.

LUTHER, Igor: A Czech, this master cameraman (*Danton, A Love in Germany*) left his native country in 1968 and worked abroad, mainly in Germany.

MARCZEWSKI, Wojciech: A young director with a very bright future. He has already made two wonderful films: *Zmory* (*Nightmares*) and *Dreszcze* (*Shivers*).

MICHALEK, Boleslaw: Critic, scriptwriter (author of my film *A Love in Germany*). I worked for twelve years with him in our Group X. He was always a priceless friend and collaborator in every area. He did advanced studies at the School of Political Science in Brussels and speaks every language, in contrast to me, who speaks none.

MUNK, Andrzej: A director, he churned out films one after the other during the 1950s and early 1960s (*Eroica, Zezowate szczescie, Cross-Eyed Happiness*), about the same generation of Poles who figured in my films. But the tone of his pictures is very different from mine: his are rationalist and ironic. His last film, *The Passenger*, remains unfinished. He was killed in an automobile accident in 1962.

OLBRYCHSKI, Daniel: Actor, who has played in many of my films (*Ashes and Diamonds, Everything for Sale, Landscape After the Battle, Birchwood,*

Promised Lands, The Young Ladies from Wilko, and others). He always aspired to be Cybulski's successor, and he has doubtless succeeded. His enormous popularity has never made him any less exacting professionally.

PAWLIKOWSKI, Adam: Critic, composer, actor. He played in *Ashes and Diamonds* and composed and played the theme for the ocarina in *Kanal.* Hypersensitive, he is also utterly winning.

PEC-SLESICKA, Barbara: Producer of all my films since the beginning of the 1970s, she is also chief of production for our Group X. Steel hands in silk gloves.

RADZIWILLOWICZ, Jerzy: Actor, "the man of marble and of iron." I discovered his talents—and that face which incarnates willpower and truth— at the Warsaw Drama School. He has also performed in my adaptations of Dostoyevsky at the Old Theater of Warsaw.

SLOWACKI, Juliusz (1809-49): Poet, one of the three "bards" of Polish romanticism. The author of numerous verse dramas, including *Fantazy.*

SOBOCINSKI, Witold: Cameraman (*Everything for Sale, The Wedding, Promised Lands*). Creative and inventive, and an excellent jazz musician, he worked with Skolimowski and Polanski.

STACHURA, Edward: Poet and prose writer, beloved of Polish youth. Always a free man, despite everything. He died tragically.

STARSKI, Allan: Set designer, who was in charge of the sets for many of my films, including: *Man of Marble, Without Anesthesia, The Young Ladies from Wilko, The Orchestra Conductor, Man of Iron, Danton,* and *A Love in Germany.* Highly professional, he combines precision with wild flights of fancy. A true filmmaker!

STAWINSKI, Jerzy: Writer, screenwriter. I owe two scripts to him: *Kanal* and *Love at Twenty.* For Munk, he wrote *Eroica* and *Cross-Eyed Love,* and for Passendorfer, *The Assassination Attempt.* As a young army officer, he took part in the Warsaw uprising. For me and all my generation of filmmakers, he was an inspiration.

WROBLEWSKI, Andrzej: The most original Polish painter of the World War II postwar period, and my friend and fellow student at the Academy of Fine Arts in Cracow. Like so many of my friends of this generation, he committed suicide.

ZANUSSI, Krzysztof: Director, author of several famous films, and the leader of that generation of Polish filmmakers who succeeded ours. Known worldwide. Rationalist, pragmatist, intellectually brilliant, a strategist, tactician, he also speaks many languages: in other words, he has all the qualities I lack.